DAY ONE TRADER

★ ★ ★ ★ ★

A LIFFE STORY

JOHN SUSSEX
WITH JOE MORGAN

A John Wiley & Sons, Ltd., Publication

Published in 2009
Copyright © 2009 John Wiley & Sons Ltd

Registered office
John Wiley & Sons Ltd, The Atrium, Southern Gate, Chichester, West Sussex, PO19
8SQ, United Kingdom

For details of our global editorial offices, for customer services and for information
about how to apply for permission to reuse the copyright material in this book please
see our website at www.wiley.com

Wiley also publishes its books in a variety of electronic formats. Some content that
appears in print may not be available in electronic books.

Designations used by companies to distinguish their products are often claimed as
trademarks. All brand names and product names used in this book are trade names,
service marks, trademarks or registered trademarks of their respective owners. The
publisher is not associated with any product or vendor mentioned in this book. This
publication is designed to provide accurate and authoritative information in regard to
the subject matter covered. It is sold on the understanding that the publisher is not
engaged in rendering professional services. If professional advice or other expert
assistance is required, the services of a competent professional should be sought.

Library of Congress Cataloging-in-Publication Data

Sussex, John, 1958–
    Day one trader : a Liffe story / John Sussex, with Joe Morgan.
       p. cm.
    ISBN 978-0-470-74173-3 (cloth)
    1. Sussex, John, 1958– 2. London International Financial Futures
Exchange. 3. Stockbrokers–England–Biography. 4. Stock exchanges–England–
Biography. 5. Finance–England. I. Morgan, Joe, 1974– II. Title.
HG5435.5.S87A3 2009
332.64'57092–dc22
[B]

                                                                    2009013324

A catalogue record for this book is available from the British Library.

ISBN 978-0-470-74173-3 (HB)

Set in 10.5 on 15 pt Sabon by SNP Best-set Typesetter Ltd., Hong Kong.
Printed in Great Britain by TJ International Ltd, Padstow, Cornwall.

CONTENTS

FOREWORD

By John Foyle

From time to time Liffe still gets requests from journalists to come to film or photograph its trading floor, and they are invariably surprised and disappointed to find that it shut almost ten years ago. Liffe's market is now fully electronic; its trading floors are history. And yet the coloured jackets, the sweat, the din, the waving arms, still vividly define what happens in financial markets in the public's mind. This is a compelling insider's story of what it was really like to trade on Liffe, and the ringside seats, fast cars, head-turning girl-friends and large houses that success could fund, which at the time made even professional footballers envious.

It is a story John Sussex is perfectly placed to tell. Entranced by what he saw on a visit to the Chicago futures markets in 1981, he became a trader on Liffe when it started up the following year, one of the 'locals' risking his own capital who provided vital liquidity to the market and an expert order execution service to the largest financial institutions.

Although John says that Liffe was 'a somewhat gentrified place compared to the bear-pits across the other side of the Atlantic', he tells the story as he saw it, warts-and-all. Colourful anecdotes sum up the fear and greed that power the markets, as well as friendship, love, and lust – here is the tale of the dealer who lost $150,000 on a single trade with a female counterpart he had simply wanted to date.

As John says, it was a young man's job. The physical demands of standing shouting in a trading pit throughout the day, before sorting out stray paperwork afterwards, meant that less than one percent of dealers were over forty. Successful floor traders, he says – drawing on over twenty years' personal experience – had to be 'mentally quick to digest the orders being fired into the market while also being tough enough to hold their own on the floor.' He describes the 'importance of assuming an aura of invincibility', crucially distinguishing that from actual, fatal arrogance. Throughout the book John's own decency shines through.

John Sussex built a thriving business of his own and, having established his reputation, was elected to the board of Liffe in May 1997. This gave him a central role in dealing with the crisis that almost overwhelmed Liffe in the late 1990s, when cheaper electronic trading became available and the exchange saw business in its German government bond contract evaporate in a single year. He found himself facing a dilemma: a man whose livelihood was founded on the trading floor, to whom other traders looked to fight their corner, and yet who could see that electronic trading was irresistible. 'The Liffe Connect platform' that Liffe invented, he writes, 'would support a new generation of technology-savvy traders in London. But for the old generation, its introduction would mark the beginning of the end.' There are poignant tales of the effect that the transition, which rescued Liffe, had on some of these: the trader who, when using a computer to trade for the first time, picked up his mouse and tried to talk to it, another dealer who did not like the change, became a fishmonger, and used his market nous to buy up cod when flocks of seagulls over Billingsgate suggested stormy weather, and poor catches, out at sea.

Throughout the book there lurks the nagging trader's fear that a sudden market move, a careless error, an unwise hire, could lead to bankruptcy. For John Sussex this moment came when in 1999, while his firm was adjusting to electronic trading, he took on a trader whose actions almost destroyed him. The episode, and the evaporation of trust it caused, are described in stomach-churning detail. He picked himself up and went on to set up a trading arcade in his home town of Basildon, where he continued to provide the benefit of his experience to younger traders at times when market volatility has surged in this, uncertain, decade.

This is a book primarily about the people who make a market and it was the size of their personalities that made it hard to believe that electronic trading could ever supersede them. John Sussex continues to believe that, in extreme circumstances, it is better to have a human making trading decisions than a computer trading programme. And, chastened by his own experience perhaps, he sounds a warning about the risk of algorithmic trading models malfunctioning and putting banks and markets under dangerous stress.

Inevitably, as with other aspects of this book, not everyone will agree with John's opinion – and after all, differences of opinion are what make markets. But there was so much more besides that made the Liffe floor market the vibrant icon of the City financial dealing markets. John's account of it makes for a gripping read.

John Foyle
Deputy Chief Executive, Liffe
June 2009

PREFACE

The book you are about to read will not teach you how to become a successful trader, it is not a biography as such and it is certainly not a self publicist book – it's a story about The London International Financial Futures Exchange (LIFFE).

A book like this could have been written by any number of traders who have traded in the pits and on the screens and I am sure they would all have a great story to tell. I was fortunate enough to have been involved from the beginning in 1982 until the exchange was sold to Euronext nearly twenty years later. During that period I was a 'day one trader', a local in the pits, ran my own brokerage company, served on the pit and floor committees, served on the Liffe Board and acted as deputy Chairman of the Automated Markets Advisory Group that helped build the electronic platform that they trade on today.

There are no pseudonyms in this book: this is a true story about real people. I have tried to tell it as it happened and really hope that I have not offended anybody mentioned as this was never my intention. I hope you find it a fascinating insight into what it was like during those ground breaking years in the City. I have tried to show how exciting and nerve–wracking it was to trade in open outcry, the characters that made the market, the super traders, business deals and politics – it's all there !

These were truly great years and I loved every minute of it, good and bad. I never had a day when I did not want to go to work and feel privileged to have made such great friends from the market – this is our story.

ACKNOWLEDGEMENTS

My sincere thanks to Joe Morgan – this book would not have been possible without him. I would also like to thank the following who have either contributed or agreed to let me write about them (there are no pseudonyms in this book): Clive Beauchamp, Darren Summerfield, Peter Lester, Nigel Bewick, David Roser, Keith Penny, Ted Ersser and David Helps who all worked with me at Sussex Futures and Alan Dickinson, Terry Crawley, Richard Crawley, David Wenman, Nigel Ackerman, Kevin Thomas, Tony Laporta, Danny Jordan, Mark Green and Roger Carlsson from the floor, also Nick Leeson, Matt Blom and Spencer Oliver.

Finally Nick Carew Hunt, James Barr and especially John Foyle from Liffe and all the staff at John Wiley & Sons for their great support. Apologies to anyone I have forgotten.

1

The Chicago Inferno

The feeling captivated me. I opened the wooden swing doors and a barrage of noise erupted from an octagonal arena the size of a vast football pitch. Scattered across the trading pits on the floor below were the yellow and red jackets of thousands of brokers and traders frantically shouting their orders into the market. Every nano-second reverberated with the sound of buy and sell orders being spewed into pits strewn with enough pieces of paper for a ticker-tape parade. The intensity of dealing on the heaving exchange floor had created its own hyperreality. What I was witnessing did not exactly appear to me in real time.

I had just caught my first glimpse of the trading floor of the Chicago Board of Trade (CBOT) and already I was hooked on the adrenaline of the pits. This was the coliseum of the financial world. It felt like standing in the greatest sporting stadium ever built by man to watch the match of the century. Brokers with physiques like American football players stood on the top steps of the floor and used brute strength to hold prime dealing positions. This was done with emphatic hand signals that I had never seen before. The gladiators in the baying pits would live or die by the numbers being churned out of the ticker-tape machines. Some would leave the floor having made tens of thousands of dollars that day. Others would 'bust out' on losses and never return again. As I felt the heat from the fluorescent lit pits I knew this was the type of place I had to be. I wanted a piece of the action.

Joe Duffy, a fresh-faced tubby young man with blond hair, was my guide for the day. A native of Chicago, he had been my counterpart in my job as a foreign exchange dealer in the City of London. My work had taken me to the windy city on a week's business trip. Squeezed into his yellow broker's jacket, Joe was doing his best to explain what was going on at the world's oldest futures and options exchange. Corn, ethanol, oats, rice and soybeans all had their own pits crammed full with hundreds of traders. Dealers were taking bets on everything from the future price of gold to the trajectory of US treasury bonds. The gaping soybean pit was huge. It fell 40 steps deep, forming a battlefield for almost 1,000 traders. A ring of yellow-jacketed clerks stood near the top steps of the pit feeding prices back to the trading booths using intricate hand signals. Financial futures and treasury bonds were traded in a dealing room adjacent to the floor. When I stepped inside it felt like waiting to get into an under-ground train in the rush hour. The place was packed so full some dealers could lift their feet off the ground and not fall. There was hardly any space for traders to move! The low ceiling and complete absence of any natural daylight only added to the claustrophobic feel of the place.

As Joe made a few quips about the antics that went on in the pits I doubt he had any idea of how spellbound I was by the whole experience. You could smell the fear and greed as sweat-soaked dealers shouted to get their orders heard. The heat from the pits made the entire exchange floor feel like a sauna! Everyone was yelling instructions at the top of their voice. In some pits, dealers were even falling over each other in a mad scramble to get orders filled. The fragments of conversation that caught my ear as I walked past were as brutal and uncompromising as the movements of the market itself. 'Don't turn your back on me I'm trading with ya ... I sold you 10 and you're damn well wearing em ... Ahhhr screw you.' Back in London, discount brokers donning top hats and three-piece suits were still strolling into the London Stock Exchange with their chins stuck up in the air. Seeing 'wise guys' in red jackets, black polo shirts and clip-on bow ties happily telling the nearest chosen enemy to 'go f**k yourself' was an eye opener.

The year was 1981. I had just turned 23 and this was my first visit to America. The cluster of skyscrapers in Chicago's downtown financial district was a long way from my home town of Basildon in Essex. That night in a watering hole near the exchange, my new drinking buddies were getting used to my unusual accent as we knocked back a few large pitchers of cold gassy American beer. It was not long before the guys wanted to hear some cockney rhyming slang, which they thought was hilarious.

After my first day's visit to the floor I was told a few war stories from the pits. A trader who suffered a heart attack on the floor had been left to die while everyone kept on trading. Before the floor observer had summoned medical help some dealers had even stuffed cards with fictitious trades into the stricken man's pockets. Unsurprisingly, physical confrontations were a frequent occurrence. In one incident a loud dispute between two traders was settled with a crunching right hand to the jaw which left the victim laid out on the pit floor. An irate floor observer leapt over and told the brawler that he had to cough up an instant $1,000 fine. When $2,000 was stuffed into his hands he appeared perplexed. Did the trader not hear that the fine was $1,000? 'I know. I'm gonna hit the son of a bitch again,' the trader replied.

My new drinking buddies were more interested to hear about what life was like in little old England. As I explained the intricacies of cricket and gave my opinion of baseball – 'just like rounders isn't?' – I could see prices coming in from the exchanges on a ticker-tape near the bar. I had already started reading the market reports of the *Financial Times* in my early morning commute before looking at the back pages of the *Daily Express* for the latest football news. Now I felt like I was in the financial world's equivalent of a sports bar. And the results from the markets never seemed to stop coming in.

I asked Joe why he still took an identity card to the bar. I was surprised when he told me that the drinking age limit in America was 21. As an Essex boy who had been drinking in pubs since the age of 15 it was all a bit strange. I still felt a bit like a kid who had just won a dream holiday. I remembered the bell boy who had greeted me the previous evening at the 5-star Hyatt hotel. He must have been a good few years older than me and the cloth of his suit was better than my own. It did feel odd giving him a tip!

I spent the next few days at the Windy City's other major dealing house, the Chicago Mercantile Exchange (CME). On the approach to the exchange I looked up at the CME's twin concrete towers which jut out confidently into the city's skyline. As I breathed in the crisp winter air I felt like I was walking the streets of a town which lived and breathed the financial markets. Thousands of people work in the financial services industry in Chicago and everyone seems to have a view on the markets. While London cabbies talk about football, the taxi drivers in Chicago give their view on where the treasury bonds futures price is heading. When I told people I was a trader it felt like saying I did the best job in the world.

The CME's trading floor was almost as big as CBOT's financial amphitheatre. I had a bird's eye view of what was going on while sitting in a broker's booth which overlooked the steps leading down to the pits. Here I punched in a few currency trades which I negotiated over the telephone with the guys from the London office. I also got to know people at the exchange and tapped their brains to find out more about the futures market. The guys in the yellow jackets were either clerks – whose job it was to collect trading cards from the pits and input trades – or telephone brokers. The traders in the red jackets were known as 'locals'. Being a local meant that you traded with your own money. In other words you could make or lose a fortune in one day. This probably explained why a fair few looked on the verge of a seizure when the action kicked off in the pits. Back home in London, the concept of people in a financial exchange trading on their own account was as alien as a City worker turning up to work wearing anything else but a white shirt. It just did not happen in 1981. And dealing was exclusively in the hands of financial institutions. The Chicago pit traders were all interested to hear about the job I did in London. I explained how I would get the best swap rates from the London cash market – which could for example be 200 points for cable Sterling/Dollar – and then make a deduction from the spot rate. So if the spot rate was 1.9525 and I deducted 200 points, the price in Chicago could be expected to stand at 1.9325. If it was different I would buy one and sell the other and when the market corrected itself I would reverse out the position and take a profit.

When my plane landed back on the tarmac of London's Heathrow airport I knew my visit to Chicago had changed my life. It was not long before I was told about plans for a financial futures exchange to be opened in London the following year and I knew I had to be there at the opening bell for the first day's trading. Never mind that I had already carved out a successful career as a foreign exchange dealer. My mind was made up.

I had not always been so sure of my destiny. Dealing millions of dollars on the global financial markets had never been suggested to me as a possible career path at my local comprehensive school in Basildon. I was born in 1958 at home in the two-bedroom council house that I grew up in and there were not any expectations on me to succeed academically. I never took the 11-plus exam and I did not know anybody at school that went on to university. The pursuit of excellence at my school was largely confined to the sporting arena. This suited me fine as a keen football player and cross country runner but at 16 I left school with just two low-grade O-Levels and eight CSE passes.

My father, John, was not disappointed in me. Just being an average student was enough for him and he never attended an open evening at the school. As one of 10 children that had been evacuated from the East End of London during the blitz he had not received much of an education himself. He was a lifelong Labour Party voter and blue collar worker who had a job at a battery factory in Dagenham. He expected me to follow in his footsteps as a factory worker. My father would play snooker every Friday night and squander his week's wages every Saturday at the local betting office. By Monday morning he would always be broke. Seeing my father give so much of the family income to the local bookmaker would have a profound effect on me years later when I became a professional trader. The only interest we shared was a love for West Ham United football club. My mother, Olive, was a housewife and part-time factory worker. While I had a happy childhood – spending many days playing football in the streets and at the local park – my younger sister, Lynne, and I never had the luxury of a holiday.

As a 15-year-old who had served as a dish washer, van boy and market stall assistant among other things I was hopeful of landing a good summer job at Basildon job centre. When I was asked what my best subject was in the classroom I said maths – an ability to be quick with figures and mental arithmetic was always my strength at school. This made me suitable material for a junior accounts clerk position. It was not until I got back home that I realised that it was a full-time job for Cocoa Merchants, a commodity brokerage firm based near Fenchurch Street in the City of London. I had only been after summer work but I thought 'what the hell, lets give it a go!'

I put on a suit which I had bought for my grandfather's funeral and got on a train to the big city. The towering buildings and bustle of the City of London's streets felt a long way from Basildon's utilitarian shopping centre. I felt a bit intimidated when I stepped through the grand entrance of Plantation House, which housed the offices of Cocoa Merchants. Inside I was greeted by a fair-skinned ginger-haired man from Essex named Bob Smith. Bob was in his late twenties. He was an Essex man from a similar background to myself. But he chose to support Leyton Orient, my football club's smaller less successful neighbour. Smith must have seen some potential, or perhaps a bit of himself in me, as he offered me the job on the spot. A quick demonstration of my mental arithmetic skills was all that I needed to pass. 'Will you be able to start next Monday?' he asked. It would be the only interview I would ever have. My career in high finance had begun.

At Cocoa Merchants I found balancing ledgers easy and I enjoyed finding my way around the accounts department. Epitomising the old ways of the City was the secretary of the firm, an elderly gentleman with balding grey hair, known as Mr Banks. He always dressed immaculately with shiny leather shoes, a black three-piece, pinstripe suit and hard-collared white shirt. He never made the effort to converse and he would watch over me as I added up thousands of numbers for the sales and purchase ledgers. Despite the rarity of a miscalculation he would never let me write anything off until everything had been re-tailed at least three times.

I would often catch a glimpse of the old man looking at me over his half-cut glasses like a disapproving schoolmaster if I was having some banter about a football match the previous night. Just one stare and I would shut up! Each evening before he left the office he would call his wife and simply says the word 'eighteen' before hanging up. This was to confirm the train from which his wife would collect him. As a young man I would ponder why he did not just call his wife if he was not taking the 'eighteen' train – he never stayed late or left early. The other young starter in the office was a university graduate called Paul James. Like myself, Paul was from the East End of London and very sharp with numbers. He sported long black hair and a beard and always dressed in the most casual suits you could find. He was also from a mixed-race background which was quite rare in the City at that time.

It did not take me long to settle into life in the City. These were the old days when trips to the square mile's many fine drinking establishments were a frequent occurrence. Never mind that my old man thought that I was not doing real man's work. Taking home £18 a week had made me rich! I made sure that I would never arrive late, leave early or take a sick day. A year later I had been promoted to a junior trader's position which involved writing up the dealing sheets and quoting Sterling/Mark for the firm's German broker, Hans Fritz. I would have done this job for nothing and it was not long before I was dealing everything from interbank deposits to certificates of deposit and Dollar/Mark.

It was around this time that I started dating my wife, Diane, a confident and attractive long-haired girl who wore blonde highlights in her hair. Diane was always the centre of attention in the office. Every evening a high-flying trader would be trying to work their magic and ask her out on a date. She worked as a telex operator to confirm my deals. I used to chat with her when everybody went to the pub but I always felt Diane was out of my league! Being a Chelsea girl from the big city and a couple of years older than me, I found her very different to the Basildon girls I had dated before. But she was very down to earth too – not at all like the Chelsea Sloane princesses for which that part of London has since become famous. We were soon married and I used my £1,500 bonus that year as a deposit to buy our first house. It was not long before we had two children. A daughter named Michelle and a son called Paul.

I loved the energy of the dealing room which was kept alive by the infectious enthusiasm of Tony Weldon, the son of the firm's owner, who was known as 'old man' Weldon. 'What's going on John? Come on. I need that price now,' he would yell at me … 'That's my boy. Keep it coming, keep it coming.' Tony was still in his late twenties and he had an ego 10 times the size of his lean 11-stone frame, topped with black slicked back hair. But I warmed to him and appreciated his enthusiastic manner. Tony's desk was located in the middle of the dealing room and he would always be jumping to his feet, instructing the traders like the conductor of an orchestra. 'Come on boys, what is going on? We are not running a bucket shop here,' he would say. The Weldon family was of Jewish descent and I suspect that they had escaped Germany after Adolf Hitler had come to power. At the time I felt I owed Tony and Bob a lot and I would later decline offers I got from headhunters as I built my reputation in the business.

The Weldon family were good friends with Bill Stern, a leading figure at General Cocoa Company Inc, a Wall Street commodity brokerage firm. When Bill's son Mitchell came over to London to learn more about the commodity business, Tony asked him to shadow me for a few days. Mitchell's dark brown wavy hair made him look a bit like Neil Diamond when he appeared in the film *The Jazz Singer*. Somehow the son of a factory worker from Dagenham and the son of millionaire Jewish Wall Street financier quickly became great friends. Tony encouraged us to go out most nights and explore the city's nightlife. I enjoyed showing Mitchell around London's

West End and introducing him to Britain's pub culture. After knocking back a few pints of lager, Mitchell liked to visit some of the more exclusive places in the capital which included some of the city's best hotels. I remember thinking how surreal it was one evening as Mitchell ordered another bottle of champagne for myself and Diane at The Savoy Hotel. The majestic Art Deco surroundings of one of London's most famous hotels seemed a long way away from my local pub in Basildon, where my mates were drinking that night.

Mitchell suggested that we go to a restaurant in Chelsea one evening. Tony had introduced him to the establishment earlier in the week and he said that he had been blown away by the place. We ended up having a great night but when the bill came we could not afford to pay. This was in the mid-seventies and I was not one of the few people that carried a Barclaycard and I did not have a cheque book to hand either. We decided to keep ordering drinks while we weighed up our options. Should we do a runner? Offer to do the washing up? In the end we asked to borrow the restaurant phone and tried to call Tony but there was no answer. By this time we were the last people in the restaurant. Luckily I was able to call Diane. She borrowed some money from her mum, jumped in a taxi and came to the rescue.

My career as a trader started to take off at about the same time as Margaret Thatcher's Britain began. My rapid journey from a pupil at the local comprehensive school to a dealer at a leading brokerage firm was exactly the sort of social mobility the new ruling Conservative Party wanted to propagate. People were being encouraged to 'get on your bike' and make their own way in the world. In the square mile, wine bars were starting to open up for business. I could almost taste the new opportunities opening up around me – and I was a young man with a big appetite. I started regularly attending lunches and after-work functions to get my name known in the City. The trappings of success that I was enjoying may sound very modest but they meant a lot to me at the time. Most importantly of all I was given my first company car, a brand new Ford Cortina worth £4,500. Owning a car is hardly the stuff a Wall Street high flyer would boast about. But it was a big deal to me. My father had never owned a car.

More responsibility would come after Cocoa Merchants was taken over by commodity brokerage firm Phillip Brothers. Whereas before I had been doing foreign exchange dealing for the firm's hedging requirements on cocoa, sugar and coffee futures I was now trading on the company's own account and executing orders for major firms. This made our firm well known with all the big banks and we started to become one of the biggest traders in the market. One of my clients was Princeton, New Jersey-based Commodities Corporation, which had tentacles in markets across the globe, managing hundreds of millions of dollars. A mystique surrounded Commodities Corporation. The trading company was renowned for using innovative trading methods and its own funds hardly ever suffered losses. Being able to do business with such a big name in finance boosted my own profile in the City. I would receive more invitations from major financial institutions to cocktail evenings and forex seminars. I was hungry for knowledge about finance and these events enabled me to further my education and expand my network of contacts.

I got a special buzz from dealing with Commodities Corporation as it had some of the superstar traders of the day including Mike Marcus, Bruce Kovner and Roy Lennox. Marcus famously had an office which housed dozens of employees built next to his beachside Malibu residence. He would call and ask for my opinion on the market. I would do my best to give the multi-million dollar speculator my view as a young man without a wealth of experience in economics or current affairs. I would explain where I had seen the flow that week. After about 10 minutes he would often make a request to buy $100 million in the opposite direction to that which I had suggested. I would later read an interview in which Marcus said that he would always make sure that he was guided by his own convictions when speaking to other traders, in an effort to ensure that he absorbed their information without getting overly influenced by their opinions. Marcus went on to retire and we did not hear from him for six months. Then out of the blue he called up and said that he was back in the business. All the aeroplanes, holidays and adventures money could buy were no match for the buzz he got from trading. 'I just can't leave it alone,' he confessed.

I had moved up the ranks on the trading floor to become second-in-command to Bob Smith who was starting to carve out a reputation as a star trader. Tony recruited Brian Marber, a specialist in financial charting, and Jim Fleming, an American from Chase Manhattan Bank. When Fleming asked Smith if he would arbitrage the currency futures in Chicago against the London cash market he refused. He was far too busy and important to devote his time to such trivial matters and the job was given to me. This would change my life.

Now I was trading financial futures and my afternoons were spent with two telephones wrapped around my ears while shouting across my desk and doing business with the big exchanges in Chicago. Rather than waiting for the telephone to ring I spent my time dealing and making calculations. You had to be mentally very quick to do arbitrage right as the job was pretty full on. But to me this was intoxicating, like a drug. My 12-hour days just flew by as I got to work on brokering million-dollar trades which ran through the firm's books like confetti. While it was a joy to work in such a fast paced environment I never lost sight of the fact that I was walking a tight-rope every day. Make one mistake as a trader and it could easily be your last. I saw this for myself first hand when a gangling lad a couple of years older than me called Gordon got an order the wrong way round one lunch time. I spotted the error as soon as I got back to my desk and reversed the position out at a big loss. While it was not my fault I felt very nervous about the whole episode but nothing was said to me. Gordon was called into the boss's office that afternoon and sacked on the spot. I never saw him again.

Trading desks are unforgiving places where the strong prey on the weak. A fresh starter can expect to be tested by experienced market veterans with a rat-like cunning for spotting an opportunity to make some easy money. Their victims are often left cursing their 'bad luck' while they find themselves looking for a nine-to-five desk job else-where. A bank trading desk is not always the most friendly place to work either. 'If you want a friend, buy a dog,' did not become a classic

Wall Street expression for nothing. One trainee dealer at a Wall Street bank found himself being completely ignored by the bond trader he was shadowing. It would be three months before the trader asked him to do anything apart from sending him on errands to buy coffee or junk food. 'I have to pop out for half an hour. If anybody calls, make sure you quote a two-tick market in five million,' ordered the bond trader before leaving the fresh-faced trainee to wait nervously by the telephone. After five minutes the receiver rang.

'Hello, and who is it zhat I am speaking to,' asked a customer from a Swiss bank.

'Err, I'm the new guy. Sorry. I mean I'm just covering the desk for a few minutes,' mumbled the trainee.

'Vell hurry up and quote me ze prices,' said the Swiss banker.

'Err … Okay six bid at eight,' said the trainee after taking a quick glance at the prices in the market.

'Stimmt. Five million mine at eight,' replied the banker.

'Oh … Well thank you.'

'No no no young man,' said the banker. 'Vere are ze prices?'

Knowing the banker was a buyer, the trainee changed the price to seven bid at nine.

'Five million mine at nine,' said the banker.

'Okay sir,' said the flustered trainee before he was interrupted again.

'No no no no young man. Vere are ze prices now?'

'Err. Eight bid at ten,' said the young dealer. He had never wanted a conversation to end so badly.

'Five million mine at ten,' said the banker.

'Err thank you sir and err …'

'No no no no young man,' interrupted the banker once again. 'Young man can you make me a price in fifteen million. Then I'm done.' All the trainee wanted to do was check the market but the customer would not let him off the telephone. This left him in a state of panic. These were his first ever trades and he had just taken on some massive positions.

'Twelve bid at 14,' said the trainee, reasoning that there was no way the customer would want to pay 14. He was right.

'Fifteen million yours at 12,' was the banker's quick reply. 'And ... Velcome to ze club my friend.' The telephone line went dead. The trainee was left to desperately check the market. He had sold treasury bonds at eight, nine and 10 before buying them back at 12 – but the market had not moved. He had been had! The treasury bonds had a value of $100,000 and each tick was worth $31.50. Selling $5 million at eight, nine and 10 before repurchasing at 12 had just cost him $14,175. When the bond trader returned to his desk he would find a distraught trainee almost lost for words when trying to explain the thousands of dollars that had vanished without a single market move.

I was told that I would be Cocoa Merchants' floor manager when the London International Financial Futures Exchange (Liffe) opened. This was my chance to get out of Bob Smith's shadow and be my own boss. It was June 1982, just three months before the Liffe floor would open, and I was hit with a bombshell. Phillip Brothers had merged with Salomon Brothers. The tie-up was sold as a marriage of 'Salomon ingenuity' and 'Philip cash', which enabled Salomon to further expand its investment banking activities. But it was bad news for me. Salomon would take responsibility for managing the floor operations at the new Liffe exchange and the only position available to me was as clerk for Ted Ersser, the man given the floor manager's job. I felt I was better than that and my pride and ego would not let me take that role. Ersser was a very different animal to myself. He would never put on a trading jacket during his entire Liffe career. A swanky grey suit with bright red braces was much more his style. I assumed that he had been public school educated but he was in fact an ex-grammar school boy who had even spent some time cheering on his beloved Chelsea in the more raucous section of the Stamford Bridge crowd during his teenage years.

Word got out that I was not happy and Heinold Commodities, a Chicago-based broker, offered me the opportunity to run their operations at Liffe. I jumped at the chance. Heinold had two seats, one booth and employed a clerk to assist me. A young polite blond woman named Clara Furse – who was destined to become chief executive of the London Stock Exchange – would work on our broker desk. Furse was strong-minded and always very professional. Handing in my notice was not an easy decision. I had two children and a £50,000 mortgage. Tony Weldon tried hard to persuade me to stay, telling me that the Liffe exchange was doomed to fail. He had already talked me out of taking a great offer from the commodity broker Marc Rich in the past. But even the advice of my trusted mentor could not stop me. I had absolutely no doubt that I had found my calling. Diane backed me and I knew there was no turning back now. It would be the beginning of a new Liffe.

2

A New Liffe

We were all gathered on the dusty wooden floorboards of an old office building on Queen Street. The place was nestled in the underbelly of the City of London and had been chosen as the venue for a trading practice session in preparation for the opening of the Liffe market. There were about 60 immaculately dressed traders. The stock brokers wore black pinstripe three-piece suits, with ties neatly folded. Some money brokers were dressed a little more casually in two-piece suits. White shirts were mandatory. The office itself looked like it had not been given a makeover since the sixties. Sunlight poured in though old-fashioned sash windows on to a bare space which would serve as a mock trading pit. Here we would practice the hand signals and dealing procedures that we needed to learn by heart for our new careers in the Liffe pits. As real money was not at stake we could all trade without fear and learn from our mistakes.

As I breathed in the dank dusty air I caught sight of what looked like a maintenance man sitting on a window sill near the radiator. Dressed in cowboy boots, ripped blue jeans and a white T-shirt, he stuck out like a sore thumb. I guessed that he may have been hanging around to fix a radiator or attend to some other menial task. When the moderator arrived we were all separated into different groups. As the name call was made I was stunned to hear the cowboy of the City answer to the name of Tony LaPorta in a gruff Chicago accent. This was no maintenance man, he was here to trade! When the bell rang to begin dealing, LaPorta moved into the centre of the mock pit like a gunslinger on a mission. In an instant he had cornered the market yelling buy and sell orders with a rapidity that left me stunned. 'Eight for 15, eight bid,' shouted the American. LaPorta had learnt his trade in the Chicago pits and he was about to give us London boys a lesson in how to trade futures and options. As I watched LaPorta go to work I thought back to my experience on the floors of the exchanges in Chicago. The intensity of those pits reminded me of a competitive sporting event. Nothing could have been further removed from a gentlemen's club of business and commerce. Now 'open outcry' dealing was about to arrive in London. The rules of the City of London were about to change forever. When Liffe opened it would no longer matter if you did not have the old school tie or an Oxbridge degree. We expected no favours and were just hungry for the opportunity to show what we could do in the new free enterprise culture of Thatcher's Britain. The Hooray Henrys were just about to meet their nemesis. This really was survival of the fittest. It didn't matter if you were from the south side of Chicago or London's East End. Those who had the skills and guile to cut it on the floor would be guaranteed success.

The Liffe exchange was located on the ground floor of the Royal Exchange, an imperious building which stands next to the Bank of England. The concrete steps and pillars of the exchange's elegant facade date back to when the building was rebuilt in the 1840s. As I walked into the members' entrance of the exchange for the first time on 30 September 1982 I felt a buzz of excitement. I had realised my ambition of being a 'day-one trader'. Inside, the fluorescent lit exchange floor bustled with about 300 traders in orange, red and blue jackets. A brief opening ceremony was overseen by Gordon Richardson, the governor of the Bank of England, before he cut a white ribbon hanging above a pulpit overlooking the floor. I felt at fever pitch as we counted down the start of trading. 'Ten, nine, eight, seven, six, five, four, three, two, one!' The bell rang and I watched a scrum of dealers scramble to trade Liffe's first ever contracts in a heap of frenetic energy.

My heart was beating fast as I looked on from my booth near the floor. I felt like a football player waiting on the substitutes' bench for an opportunity to come on to the field of play for the big match. Now all I needed was a rush of orders from Heinold's broking desk and I could dive into the fray. After 15 minutes I was still waiting for my first order. I was just a spectator. When the Smith Brothers traders came back to the booth nearby to hand in their trading cards they looked like they had been pushed through a hedge backwards. 'Man it's murder in there,' said Danny, a bearded ginger-haired American dealer. His girlfriend, Steph, had been going at it full pelt in the pits as well. She was a typical native of Chicago and would be described in a newspaper the next day as a 'gum-chewing lady with a voice like a klaxon'. I could tell that they all had been loving the experience though and I could not wait for the telephone to ring any longer. 'Call me if you get an order,' I told my clerk. 'I am going in.'

The feeling was electric as I walked the 30 feet from my booth to the Eurodollar pit. I had a flashback to standing on the terraces at a big football match as I waited outside a scrum of traders who were dealing frantically. A polite 'excuse me' would get me nowhere so I got to work at barging my way through to get myself in a position where I could trade. It all felt a bit out of control. Sometimes I could not even tell if my feet were still touching the ground.

As I stumbled on the floor I began to focus my mind on what I had to do. I looked up at the big electronic Ferranti board which displayed the bid and offer prices to make a last-minute check on what was trading. Bid and offer numbers represented prices at which other traders were willing to buy (bid) or sell (offer) futures contracts. Everyone appeared to be buying sevens. What looked like the last seven available was being offered by a red-jacketed dealer standing just five feet away. 'Buy one,' I shouted. 'Sold!' I had just done my first trade! 'Who are you?' he yelled. 'HNO [Heinold],' I replied. But he could not hear me so I pulled up the badge of my red jacket before receiving a thumbs-up to acknowledge the trade. After double-check-ing to confirm that I had paid seven for one contract I got to grips with scribbling details of the trade on to my dealing card while trying to stay on my feet in the crammed pit. The market was now trading at seven bid. 'One at eight,' I shouted at the top of my voice, thrust-ing my palms outwards to show that I was a seller. 'One at eight. One at eight!' I felt a hand nudge my shoulder. 'Buy it'. The deal had been done and I had made a tidy $25 profit. I felt elated as I worked my way out of the pit. This was everything that I had hoped it was going to be. While trying to look cool and composed, inside I felt like a Cheshire cat grinning from ear to ear.

I quickly became intoxicated by the feeling of trading on the floor. Dealing was explosive and in your face. Trades were often done through a force of will, using a loud voice while throwing out hand gestures with the repetition of a fighter shadow boxing combinations. Open outcry could not be compared to the insipid world of trading over the telephone. When the market got busy I felt like I was at the centre of a vortex of whirling trades. I quickly began to learn how to navigate this new world and found myself being able to gauge price movements by the intensity of the voices in the pit. This was as close as I was ever going to get to being a professional footballer and I loved it. I woke up each morning bristling with excitement at the prospect of another day's work. The tough physical and mental chal-lenge of doing the job only seemed to add to my enthusiasm.

All the action in the pits was being driven by Salomon Brothers, which controlled the lion's share of dealing in London's Eurodollar market. This was helping Ersser quickly make a name for himself – doing a job which I felt rightfully should have been mine. Smith Brothers was using the talent that it had recruited from Chicago to make its presence felt in the market. Dealers from the firm wore badges which bragged 'It's hard to be humble when you're from Chicago.' It did not take me long to realise that apart from the odd small order Heinold would not have much business for Liffe. I did not feel cheated as the firm had never promised that it would be dealing large volumes before I joined. But this meant that if I wanted to make money on futures and options I would have to be extra smart. Dealers from Chicago were already complaining that the market was dominated by big commercial interests which made it tough for the small band of locals on the exchange that were speculating with their own money.

I spotted an arbitrage opportunity between London and Chicago in the Eurodollar market and persuaded Ulrich von Schilling, the managing director of Heinold, to provide me with a 20 lot trading limit with the CME. I doubt he had any clue what I was going to do with these trading limits but he trusted me. My plan was to sell or buy contracts in London when the prices were expensive or cheap relative to those offered in the Chicago pits. Arbitraging currencies at Cocoa Merchants had already put me ahead of the curve. My strategy was earning me a steady profit and the other dealers on the floor did not seem to realise what I was doing. They assumed that I was just filling orders.

Phil Barnett, managing director of the futures operation at Smith Brothers, one day asked how I was doing. When I told him that I was 35 ticks up for the day which equated to a $750 profit he was stunned. 'How the hell did you do that?' he asked. 'I only saw you trade a couple of times.' He was all ears as I explained to him how I carried out my arbitrage strategy. Barnett told me that he wanted some of this business and asked me to be his broker into the Chicago pits. I agreed and within a few days all the American traders at Smith Brothers had adopted my arbitrage strategy. I would check the prices trading in Chicago over the telephone before hand signalling them to Smith Brothers traders in the pits. This enabled them to react quicker to market moves than rival dealers in the pits, thereby giving them an edge. These guys were the biggest personalities in the market and they rattled through hundreds of trades each day. I charged them $17.50 a round trip commission and they were still making good money. It did not take too long for rival traders to see what we were doing. But our guys were prepared to take on greater risks and were quicker and more aggressive. This made it very difficult for rivals to compete.

Dealing on the exchange grew steadily with average daily volumes reaching 7,000 by the end of the first year. But the jury was still out on whether the market would succeed. It was obvious to everyone who worked at the exchange that a good few people in the City wanted us to fail. Not that this mattered to us. It was a fantastic feeling to be involved in such a new market and this created a great camaraderie among everyone on the floor. At lunch time and in the evening we would spill on to the City's streets wearing our brightly coloured jackets and take over the pubs around the exchange. The Cock and Woolpack was transformed from being a quiet empty boozer nestled behind the Royal Exchange on Finch Lane to the brewery's most profitable pub after Liffe opened. Business was also good at the Jamaica Inn. Hugh Morgan, who leased a seat from Heinold on the exchange, and other more experienced dealers could be found in Simpson's Tavern. Hugh was in his late thirties which made him a bit old to carve out a successful career in the pits. He wore thick-rimmed tortoiseshell glasses which poked out in front of his blonde silver hair. Hugh always sported an authentic Hermes tie which matched an expensive suit, making him appear like the classic stock broker type. Some of the best locals liked to enjoy a daily dose of bubbly at The Greenhouse, located just by the traders' entrance of the exchange. The tiny champagne bar had been the almost exclusive preserve of London Stock Exchange members before Liffe opened its doors and provided the establishment with a more hard-drinking clientele.

Whether Liffe would remain a permanent part of the City's square mile or not was still in the balance after its first year of trading. I desperately wanted the market to succeed which gave me an almost fanatical focus on doing my job to the best of my abilities. After the first year I had generated £250,000 in gross commission and trading profits. Early on in this successful period, Hugh had asked me to trade for him and I had quickly made an excellent return on the money he gave me to trade with. While Hugh had attended Liffe's pit trading sessions and exams he had not really participated. The exams took place in an office in Old Jewry. Most people who attended had a financial background – attendees included a mixture of com-modity brokers, stock brokers, money brokers and bankers – but very few knew much about financial futures. The demographic of the new exchange consisted of young hungry dealers looking for their big break in the City and experienced bankers who were relaunching their careers at the new venture. In the months before the exchange opened the need to get hundreds of traders on to the floor meant it was quite easy to pass the exams. A knock-on effect of this was to give people like myself who had left school at 16 a shot at being successful traders. Some would grab this chance.

Hugh on the other hand had already made enough money to retire in Bermuda for a year. He had come a long way from his days as a school teacher before he got his big break in the City. He no longer had the desire you need to make it from scratch on the Liffe floor. After registering for the training sessions he would usually sneak off to the pub, the natural milieu of many a South Wales native. Here you could often find him in animated discussions on the performance of the Welsh national rugby team. He loved to get into heated debates at the bar and he would always have a rugby story to tell to his circle of friends that congregated alongside him. It was over a pint in the basement of the Simpson's Tavern that Hugh and I had first formed our partnership. I agreed straightaway. I liked Hugh and always enjoyed his company. He always showed great confidence and belief in me.

It was not long before Hugh asked me to leave Heinold and set up a new partnership with him. This was a big step to take even though I had done so well in my first year of trading. I would lose most of my commission income and as a local I would not be able to use the arbitrage strategy which had served me so well at Heinold. I also was on a nice package for the time of £30,000 a year and had a wife, a mortgage and two children to support. This made me hesitate about the partnership but I knew Hugh believed in my abilities as a trader and I trusted his business acumen. Hugh used his connections in the City to arrange for Coast Investment & Development Company, a Kuwait-based investment bank, to provide me with a guaranteed salary and profit share while he became their fund manager. We traded under the name Coast & Partners.

Hugh and I quickly proved ourselves to be a winning team. My strategy on the floor was becoming increasingly successful and I was starting to pick up floor brokerage business, whereby another firm would ask a local such as myself to execute trades on their behalf. Salomon Brothers, for example, had no traders at all at the time. I was usually paid about £1.50 a lot which meant if I could fill a couple of hundred lots a day I would earn a lucrative income stream.

The fact that Hugh spent most of the time in the pub while I was working flat out on the trading floor did not bother me at all. The last thing I wanted was anyone interfering with what I was doing on the trading floor. I had quickly developed my own way of doing things. Hugh provided the finance and I did the trading and broking. Like many people in the City at that time, Hugh and I conducted all our business at the pub and it was over a few pints that we agreed on Hugh's plan to buy out Coast & Partners (the partners were Phil Barnett, Hugh and myself). We became Morgan Sussex Ltd in 1984. Now I was a pure local trader with no corporate backing. But there would be no limits on my earning potential either. The partnership with Hugh meant that I would take a greater share of the profits but would be responsible for any losses and I would have no safety net if things went wrong. The wheeler dealer valley boy from South Wales and the hungry young trader from Basildon had thrown their chips onto the Liffe table in the biggest gamble of my life.

3

What's in a Name?

The fortunes of Morgan Sussex depended on my ability as a trader. I felt that I had to win a victory in the pits every day. The yelling and shouting around me in the bustling arena of the Royal Exchange floor might as well have been a baying crowd of vocal sports fans. Every time I made a winning trade the cacophony of voices felt like a rapturous applause that only I could hear. One of the things I feared the most at the beginning was being hit with a potentially ruinous out trade. An out trade occurred when a trader thought that he had made a trade with a dealer – for example selling five lots – when in fact that dealer had done the trade with someone else. This left the trader thinking that he had sold five lots when no transaction had taken place. The trader would be left having to reach an agreement with the other dealer on the out trade, which could cost him thousands of pounds if an abrupt market move had taken place.

I only let positive thoughts enter my mind during the early days of the venture, confident that a hard work ethic and passion for the job would be enough to ensure success. Living and breathing the futures markets 24/7 had quickly become a way of life. A professional athlete would have found it hard to match my dedication to the job – leaving aside an appalling diet that consisted of large amounts of crisps, chocolates, biscuits and occasional food binges after working a day in the pits without eating. Luckily, I could consume a mountain of junk food without putting on an ounce of weight. I remained as lean as a bean pole throughout my career as a trader.

I rose at six o'clock every morning, my thoughts clear having not consumed a drop of alcohol the previous evening. Tea and a biscuit served as breakfast before I caught the two minutes past seven train from Basildon to Fenchurch Street. After reading the latest financial news on my journey to work I would plug into the Reuters news wires at the exchange, look at the interbank cash markets and scan the prices from the previous night's close in Chicago. At 8:30 the bell rang to begin trading and I would work flat out, more often than not without even taking lunch. When I did grab a sandwich roll in the exchange's canteen – which overlooked the trading floor – my lunch break would last no longer than 10 minutes. Then I would stay on my feet trading non-stop until the final bell at quarter past four. Time after the market closed was spent totting up the day's dealing positions while keeping an eye on Chicago, especially if I still had some open positions. As these were the days before everyone had mobile phones, I would place a stop order with my broker at the CME to protect myself against any sudden market moves before leaving the exchange. My pager fed me the latest market news on the train journey back to Basildon. Another call would be made from home to close any positions in Chicago a few minutes before the exchanges closed at eight o'clock. Holding positions overnight was gambling. If an earthquake or similar cataclysmic event took place overnight my fate would be out of my hands. After a meal and a quick shower I watched the nine o'clock news on the television before going to bed at about 10 o'clock. A good night's sleep was vital for staying mentally sharp. For some reason I never had enough time in a day to cram in nightclubbing in London's West End. Well, you are what you are I suppose.

Sure enough, my commitment started to reap rewards. Dealing volumes funnelling through the business grew steadily which enabled us to sponsor other traders. Cable Bob, a senior trader from Midland Bank, became our first signing. His name was Bob Mattinson but to everyone on the floor he was Cable Bob, owing to his obsession with tracking the Dollar/Sterling cable as a guide when trading the gilt futures contract. He had been a commodity trader before his career at Liffe and he was the quintessential English gentleman, having the appearance of a good-looking Prince Charles. Morgan Sussex leased him a seat and deposited £25,000 at our clearer as a guarantee to cover any losses that he made. In return we took 40% of the profits that he earned.

Morgan Sussex soon had a good team of traders. Cable Bob was followed by Darren Summerfield, Adam Rosenberg and Owen Bowler. I became the most profitable trader in a close-knit group of dealers which continued to make modest steady returns. A desk in the office of First Options of Chicago – which had operations in a building opposite the Royal Exchange – served as the Morgan Sussex head-quarters although the Simpsons Tavern was known as our branch office because so much of our business was done there. We might not have made the big league yet but we were making money and Hugh was happy. Another recruit was Andy Hughes, whose fluffy hair and pointed nose quickly earned him the name Llama. The nicknames traders picked up were part and parcel of the banter on the floor. Dealers either put up with it or quit. The pits could be unforgiving places and letting your guard down just once would be enough to leave you carrying an uncomplimentary nickname for the rest of your trading life. The perfect example of this would be the moniker 'Deutsche Mark' given to a young dark haired broker named Darren. While working as a junior trader for Tulletts, a London-based money broker, Darren was given two orders for the currency pit to buy four lots at the market price and sell three lots at the market price. Dutifully, he walked into the Deutsche Mark pit and asked a market maker from Midland Bank what was on offer. Two bid at seven was the quote. 'Okay sell three at two and buy four at seven,' he earnestly replied. This was a big mistake. He should have crossed three at five and bought one at seven, providing both customers with better fills and not just giving money to the market maker. Word of his error quickly spread around the floor and Darren soon picked up the nickname Deutsche Mark. No matter that he later became a very good order filler, Deutsche Mark Darren would have to live with the unflattering sobriquet of an unreliable dealer for the rest of his career. Not that this would be a barrier stopping Deutsche Mark from obtaining the trust of his peers in the pits. In fact, he was once given the responsibility of organising Tulletts' Christmas dinner. He had the task of phoning up a fashionable restaurant in London's West End to book a table for the meal. When asked what was on the menu he was told beef, turkey and venison.

'What is venison?' queried Deutsche Mark
'Deer Sir,' was the curt reply of the restaurateur.
'Oh. Well I don't give a f**k anyway, Tullet is paying!' said Deutsche Mark before slamming the phone down.

Appearances certainly did not go unnoticed on the trading floor. A young dealer with long fair hair who was a bit flash turned up for work one day wearing an earring. This was a big mistake. It was not long before one of the bigger traders in the pits spotted his fashion accessory and started calling him Doris. Soon everybody in the pit was calling him Doris. He never wore an earring again but the damage had been done. Nobody would remember his real name from that day onwards. Fortunately, he had a thick skin and just accepted his new name with grace.

Each day you would hear dealers answer to names which had their own story like BFG (which could be short for big friendly giant or big fat git, depending on how you saw the big man), Cabbage, Crazy, Fraggle, Grebbo, Gripper, Gurner, Lardy, Lurch, Mad Dog, Psycho and Simply. Some would even change the trading badges on their jackets to match their nicknames. I think I got off lightly as far as nicknames went. I was known at Johnny Red in the early days because I quoted prices in months known as 'the red months'. Most traders embraced their nicknames. What often started out as just a joke at someone's expense became signatures of some of the floor's most endearing personalities.

One of the biggest personalities on the floor was a trader called Richard Crawley, who went by the name Dogsy. He had the demeanour of a disruptive school boy in the eighties children's television programme Grange Hill. Many dealers would remember him for an ungainly, fast-paced walk which he used to get quickly around the pits. Running was not allowed on the floor. His speed walk looked all the more comical, given that he was a big well-built bloke from South London and definitely not the most agile chap in the pits. His walk became known as the 'Dogsy walk'. As Dogsy made his way around the floor other dealers would time his laps and chant 'hey, hey, hey ...' Dogsy even devised his own snooker game in the pits in which he would walk around the pit as if it was a snooker table, lining dealers up with an imaginary cue. Dogsy would ape chalking his cue and pretend that he had 'screwed back' before taking the next shot. Sometimes he would even project himself like a human cannon ball to get his shot right. Hit a red-jacketed local and that was one point. Ram a yellow-jacketed runner into the steps near the pit and that was two points. The green jackets of Allied Irish Banks scored three. Knock a brown jacket from Gridley's out of the pit ring and that was four points. The blue of Barclays earned five, the pink of Phillips & Drew six and the black-jacketed Bache brokers were walking seven-point targets. Not everyone appreciated Dogsy's sense of humour and he once walked around the exchange floor sporting two black eyes. His attacker had probably resorted to violence after being made to look like a clown by the South London boy's sharp wit.

A contender for Dogsy's crown as Liffe's court jester was a young man called Paul Johnson who worked in the short sterling pit. He went by the name Batesy owing to a passing resemblance to Anthony Perkins, the actor who played Norman Bates in the film Psycho. Batesy's favourite trick was to make a daring lap of the dealing floor, walking at a fast pace around the second highest step surrounding the pits. In a re-enactment of the motorcycle 'wall of death', Batesy would get all the order fillers to stand on the top step and act as a wall leaving the second step down completely free while the rest of the traders would step down to the bottom. The dozen or so steps circling the floor were very steep and all the dealers would cheer and clap as he made his way around.

Trading was a young man's game. One man bucking this trend was a grey-haired ageing dealer at a major clearing bank. Whenever he came down to the floor to trade he knew that he was well out of his depth. When he held his trading card his hand would violently shake, such was the terror he felt on his journey into the pits. One dealer thought that his card resembled a 'cardiac chart'. It would be almost impossible to read a word on his dealing cards and the old man soon got the nickname Kellogg. Every time he was on the floor he got the corn flakes, shakes.

An American trader who started work on the Liffe floor made the mistake of telling his new colleagues that he was a 'big fish' in Chicago. The next thing he knew, everyone was calling him Tuna. Whenever he walked into a different pit he would be greeted with football style chants of 'Tuna, Tuna, Tuna …' The American would have to get used to this name for the rest of his trading life. Not all dealers handled being given a nickname in the same way. One trader discovered that his less than chiselled good looks had earned him the uncomplimentary nickname Gurner. He looked like a prop forward in a rugby team. But he never minded the name calling. When dealers shouted Gurner at him he would often respond with a smile. Gurner would later tell me that he had a tremendous feeling that he belonged after he had been given a name on the floor. 'I really miss it. The best time of my life,' he said. His response contrasted starkly with another dealer who became almost suicidal after he picked up a less than flattering nickname. When the brokers who started the name calling refused to stop he sought legal advice and tried to prosecute those involved for harassment in the workplace. Of course, receiving letters from a solicitor galvanised the brokers to use the nickname as much as possible and it was not long before the sensitive dealer was looking for work elsewhere.

Being self-confident with a quick-thinking mind were not just important qualities needed for success on the trading floor. Having a sharp wit was a good weapon to have when the banter got fierce. On one occasion, a top trader in the Italian Government Bond (BTP) pit chose to pick on a young broker named Ben who was filling orders for me.

'Oi Ben, why are you so fat?' he mocked.
'Because every time I shag your Mrs she makes me a bacon sandwich,' replied Ben.

The floor erupted in laughter and even the bully had to smile at the young lad's chutzpah. Rather than melt with embarrassment young Ben had fired one back at the top trader in the BTP pit.

Being a new boy in the pits could be tough. One of the ritual initiation ceremonies was to stick a folded trading card under the collar at the back of a clerk's yellow jacket. The only way a new boy would start to find out about this childish gag is when he noticed other dealers shouting 'shark' whenever he approached them. The card stuck under his collar would look a bit like a shark fin. This could be quite a bewildering experience for some who would not have a clue about what was going on. Others would even try to play along and join in shouting shark. The eventual discovery of the paper fin pegged on to the back of their jacket would result in acute embarrassment. Another popular trick was a practice known as 'spurring'. Dealers would cut two trading cards into the shape of cowboy spurs and stick them together. When the pits were slow a new boy on the floor would be distracted while the two paper spurs were sellotaped to the back of his shoes. As he walked around the pit he would hear clapping, the pounding of feet and he would be loudly greeted with the words 'yeeeeeee ha!' wherever he went.

Another prank was known as the 'long waited option'. A new runner would be sent into the options pit and told to ask dealers for a price in the long waited option. This was a bit like asking a decorator's mate to get some stripped paint. The hapless runner would be told to stand in the corner and wait while everyone surrounding him would watch to see how long it took for him to twig that he was the victim of a practical joke. After asking when the order was coming in a couple of times – only to be told to keep waiting – most would walk back to their dealing booth and be greeted with a torrent of laughter. The record for the longest waited option stood at four hours and was set by a runner known as Plug.

Any visitors to the floor could expect to run the gauntlet of shouting brash dealers. Being a little different in any way would be an invitation to get a barrage of insults from some tough and sharp-witted guys. An attractive female stepping on to the floor would be greeted with cries of 'beaver' wherever she went. Young women would look so uncomfortable and embarrassed. As time went on people would be scared to go on to the floor. Just like at a football match when the crowd is buzzing, the pits could also produce some great comical moments. If you suffered any misfortune you could soon find yourself becoming the object of ridicule. I broke my thumb once and had it heavily bandaged. When I returned to the Eurodollar pit after my lunch break and asked what was on offer I was greeted by sixty traders waving a hand signalled price with pieces of trading cards wrapped around their thumbs.

On one occasion a trader who had left for a better job was forced to make a humbling return to the dealing floor. He had been tempted to leave Hill Samuel, a British merchant bank, for Dean Witter Reynolds, an American brokerage firm, by the offer of a higher salary and a BMW company car. But the demands of working at a fast-paced broker were too much and the move had not worked out. This left him swallowing his pride and asking his former employer if he could return to his old job. When he made his first hesitant steps back on to the short sterling pit floor he looked up to see his old dealing pals spontaneously erupt with a vocal rendition of Elvis Presley's 'Return to Sender'. Only the lyrics had been changed to Return to Samuel. 'Return to Samuel, pay unknown, no BMW, no car phone ...'

Having a punt on the horses was a popular pursuit among many floor traders. Dogsy and a few of his mates in the gilt pit would regularly have a flutter on the races. A tall slim broker called Legsy would relay commentary from a nearby booth when a big race meeting was held. If Dogsy had been given a good tip he would tell other dealers who would then let the whole pit know if a winning bet was made. An earnest young broker who was new on the floor once asked Dogsy if he would put a bet on for him. Dogsy thought this was a great opportunity to play a prank on the new boy.

'No problem, how much do you want to put on?' he asked.
'I was thinking about £ 50,' said the clerk.
'Don't waste my time,' said Dogsy. 'Let's make it a monkey and I will do it for you.'
'Okay,' agreed the clerk, who must have felt like a rabbit looking into the headlights of a fast-approaching car. Dogsy also went by the name 'minder' and you would not want to have a disagreement with him over money.
'We are all on Gullible Boy to win in the 3.30 at Newmarket,' said Dogsy. 'I'll place the bet on my account for you.'

Afterwards the new boy quickly found out that a monkey was £ 500. Now he was in a state of high anxiety sweating on the result of the race like his life depended on it. The sum of £ 500 was probably more than a month's take home pay. After a while he could not take it any more. That bet had to be cancelled! He approached Dogsy and meekly made his request, praying that he would be met with a sympathetic ear. 'NO WAY,' said Dogsy. 'You're having a laugh mate. I have already put the bet on!'

Later that afternoon, all the dealers gathered around a booth at the edge of the gilt pit to hear Legsy give a running commentary of the 3:30 race. The young clerk stood nervously among the spectators. 'They are under starters orders and they are off!' shouted Legsy before hurtling into a gripping commentary of the race for the next two minutes. Soon the race was reaching its climax. 'Gullible Boy is now two lengths ahead with two furlongs to go!' said Legsy as he continued his commentary at a breakneck pace. By now the young clerk was jumping up and down like a man possessed. All the dealers around him were cheering loudly as the race entered its last stages. 'Go on my son,' he yelled at the top of his voice. 'It is Gullible Boy, and still Gullible Boy as we reach the finish line,' continued Legsy before the race suddenly took a new twist. 'Oh no! Coming up fast on the rails is the Joker. The Joker is coming on strong. And at the line it is ...'

'Who? Who won?' cried the clerk in a state half way between euphoria and despair.

'The Joker wins, Gullible Boy is second,' confirmed Legsy.

The despondent clerk's head was now in his hands. He slumped on to the floor, looking like a football player who had just lost in the FA Cup Final. Eventually he opened his eyes to see his nemesis standing in front of him. 'Have you got my money?' asked Dogsy. Before the clerk could answer, everyone around him burst into hysterical laughter. It would take a few moments before the truth dawned on him. There had been no 3:30 race at Newmarket.

To an outsider the floor would look a harsh and intimidating place. But the pioneering spirit that we all felt when the exchange first opened had grown to make us feel a bit like a band of brothers. The ceaseless banter went from the trading floor to the pub and back again. Ian Dury, the cockney singer-songwriter of Blockheads fame, spent a week in the Bank of America booth observing the antics which went on. He used this experience to write material for Serious Money, a West End musical about the Liffe exchange. I joined a big group of traders who sat in the front row to watch the opening night's performance of the show. Here we watched actors transform the hand signals and brokerage jargon that we used every day into Ian Dury's rap songs. A song about a dealer trying to cancel an errant order into the market – which went 'in you c**t oh out oh f**k it' – captured the floor's patois about right. The cast knew we were watching as they performed in front of us and while it was obvious that they were taking the mickey at least we could laugh at ourselves. We had all met up in the bar before the show and the barman asked one trader if he wanted to place an order for the interval. He calculated that there were 48 of us and we would require two drinks each so he ordered 96 pints of lager. When we returned at the interval to my disbelief all the pints of beer were stacked up across the bar. I had never seen anything like it!

The City of London was inhabited by a new breed of trader and it needed to get used to it. We were breaking new ground and it felt great. We knew that across the road from the Royal Exchange at the London Stock Exchange (LSE) stock brokers were slitting each other's throats in a gentlemanly sort of way just as they had done for generations. On our lunch break we would often pass dealers from the LSE. The disdainful glances we sometimes got seemed all the more pathetic given the shock waves that the explosion in derivatives dealing was already sending through the capital markets. I never felt at all embarrassed while wearing the coloured jacket on the street or in the pub. In fact, wearing the jacket felt like a badge of honour. It would not be too long before the News at Ten started sending the cameramen to the Liffe floor rather than the LSE when a big financial news story broke.

4

Laws of the Jungle

It was a busy day in the pit. Orders were flying in thick and fast. This was bread and butter stuff for the Eurodollar arbitrage between London and Chicago. I had been filling orders for Kate, a clerk in a booth nearby. She had a phone permanently wrapped around her ear as she listened to the latest prices at the CME. Her job was to hand signal orders into the Eurodollar pit when prices in Chicago moved. Speed was of the essence. I had just signalled back to the booth that 200 were on offer at seven. Seconds later, Kate was frantically waving at me. She had done well to get my attention as I stumbled around the crowded Eurodollar pit. As Kate shouted my name she pulled her hand towards her body with the palm facing inwards. She wanted me to buy all 200! I got to work buying all the offers in the pit, gobbling them up in double-quick time. 'Buy them, buy them … Buy them!' I must have dealt with about 20 traders before hand signalling back to Kate that I had paid seven for 198. This was a very big order in the early days of the exchange. Yet instead of confirming the trades she just blanked me. What was she doing? 'Kate, I paid seven for 198,' I yelled. 'John, I never gave you an order,' was her stunned reply. 'I wanted you to come over here and check a trade which we had done earlier.' Panic hit me like a bucket of cold water thrown in my face. That was $5,000 a tick, a fortune to me at the time as I had only just started trading as a local. The prices could easily have gone down five or 10 ticks. Luckily I managed to keep my cool and offload the trades without suffering any losses. Make a split-second mistake like that on the floor and you could see your career evaporate before your eyes.

Having the intuition and necessary speed of thought to make the right decision when under intense pressure was part and parcel of being a pit trader. Dealers needed a cool head, good hand–eye coordination and a loud voice. Just being able to use your voice to get noticed was not enough though. Orders had to be communicated in a controlled way. Let any sign of panic come into your voice and other traders would soon be circling around you like vultures. The mental toughness to deal with the in-your-face tactics of intimidation used by rival pit traders was vital. Traders who lacked the speed and aggression needed to regularly make trades would not last a week in the pits. A similar skill set is arguably needed by professional athletes. The stereotype of a bunch of barrow boys jumping around and bluffing their way to a fortune could not be further from the truth.

Watch a fiercely competitive sports match and you will often see people cheating. The trading floor had its fair share of dirty tricks too. Unscrupulous dealers tried to get an edge by any means possible. Innocent misunderstandings were by no means the only peril that you had to watch out for. There were rumours that some locals who filled orders in the pits would make secret payments to the floor managers to get a bigger slice of business. Being a floor trader meant that you were dependent on hand signals for the execution and delivery of trading orders and this system itself was open to abuse. Anyone standing on the top steps of the pit could see hand signalled orders coming into the market. The unwritten rule was that a trader should let a broker fill his order before he bought or sold for his own account. But some locals would jump on an order coming into the pit and buy it before offering it a tick higher to the broker. This was known as front running. A broker who had been told to buy an offer from his customer would have to say that he had missed it. This would cost him a commission and make him look bad. An enraged broker would feel the need to tell the local a transgression had taken place. Yelling 'you f**king thieving bastard' usually did the trick. The local would tell him that he had just been too slow before the pair inevitably squared up to each other in a pushing and shoving match. It would be left to bystanders nearby to break up the altercation. However, only a minority of locals would front run and bad brokers used the practice as an alibi after misquoting the market or being too slow. 'The locals bought them,' would be the catch-all excuse. Good brokers would refuse to trade with unethical locals which stopped them from getting stung.

The law of the jungle ruled in the pits. The weak and incompetent did not last long. If another dealer crossed you, he would pay for it. If, for example, I had been bidding fives for JP Morgan and another broker failed to split his trades with me – choosing instead to sell 50 lots at five just to the two traders standing next to him – I would have to make him know about his mistake. Yelling at him 'What the f**k is wrong with this side of the pit?' would be a starting point but it would be no consolation when JP Morgan asked how many I had bought. I would have to say none and get a look which said: what are we paying you for? Make your presence felt or we will get somebody else to fill our paper. If I got an order to sell 50 on the bid later on I would make sure that everyone that was bidding got something – I might fill two trading cards dealing with fifteen different traders – except the dealer who had not split his trades with me the previous time. Afterwards I would do the rounds checking my trades. 'So that is two with you, five with you ... Oh, and none with you mate (to the guy who had missed me out earlier).' He would soon get the message. I would be the first person that he traded with the next time.

Sometimes physical force was needed to get yourself noticed. When more than 500 people were clamouring to make a trade at the same time dealers would not always respond when you tried to execute an order. Grabbing another dealer by the scruff of his neck was a good way of making sure he had your undivided attention. Disputes often erupted over a trade when a dealer had not heard somebody make a buy order. A dealer who had been ignored would get right in the face of the other trader and shout: 'I f**king sold those first.' 'Tough, I never heard you,' would be a common reply to which a dealer may respond: 'You f**king useless t**t, you're a f**king dead man. I know where you live!' This type of verbal confrontation was a daily occurrence which would sometimes lead to punches being thrown.

The aggressive nature of pit trading made it a tough place for women. Not having the physical size and strength to hold a dominant position on the floor left many women struggling when trading got fierce. While those who worked for major companies on the floor would have the support of colleagues around them, women who worked for small dealing firms would often find themselves being literally squeezed out when some big orders came into the pits. Even well-built men would be knocked out of the pits by dealers scrambling to take on big market orders.

Whoever traded in the pits could expect to be tested. I once had a tough confrontation with Mark Green, when he was the biggest trader in the Eurodollar pit. Green was a man born with all the gifts a trader needed. Loud, cocky and incredibly self-confident, the fair-haired Green had a lean physique which betrayed a hunger to beat every other dealer out of sight. Using tactics of intimidation to force dealers to trade at his price was part and parcel of his weaponry on the floor. I was working as an order filler when Green spotted me obtain an order to pay eight by JP Morgan when they were eight offered and very lightly bid. In no time, Green was in my face making it very clear that he was eight offered and expected me to trade most of the contracts with him. I just smiled and told him that I was seven bid. I considered it my job to get an improved fill for the customer whenever I could. After all, this was the job that my customers were paying me to do and if I kept giving them lousy fills the bank would use someone else and I would not get paid. My response enraged Green. He would often force brokers to trade with him by spoofing the market. A spoofer used large quantities of bids or offers to create the illusion that there was more demand to buy or pressure to sell than the 'true' bids and offers represented. A spoofer manipulated the weight of the numbers to force the market to go in his favour. I refused to budge as Green became more aggressive. He told me that if I did not pay up in two minutes flat he would buy all the eight offers, which would really mess me up. The situation became like two stags butting antlers. I just stood my ground. I was seven bid and knew the true value as I could see the treasury bonds were looking weak and felt confident that the bid would soon trade. Green knew this as well which was why he wanted me to pay up. It felt a bit like somebody trying to mug you. Do you stand your ground or give the guy your wallet? Most corporate order fillers had the attitude that the wallet might as well be passed over. After all, it was not their own money at stake. But I was never going to do this. Holding my ground ensured that my customer obtained an improved fill on the order. Green found out that I was not to be messed with and I probably earned his respect that day.

The ethos on the floor was not completely cut-throat, especially in the early days. If a genuine mistake had occurred, dealers would usually help each other out. If, for example, a broker had over-bought on an order when trading to split a trade up locals would try to let the broker off on some contracts and cancel or reduce their number of trades. A broker with any sense would make sure that the locals who had helped him out got a good deal the next time they traded. Brokers were also known to stop out a local on the last 10 lots of his order. For example, just bidding for 40 when he needed 50. If someone came in and sold all the bids before a local could react, he would lose money. But if a broker had held back 10, the local would be guaranteed not to lose

Having allies on the floor could be a great help. Once a good friend of mine was filling a trade for Exco, a large money broker. He was buying all the offers and I was desperately trying to sell to him for my own account. To my dismay, he kept on ignoring me. This made me angry until I realised that he was doing it deliberately and probably had a big market order. Sure enough, he took the market up three ticks before turning to me and buying 20. Then he told the pit: 'I'm done.' He knew if he had a problem in the future I would help him out. I would frequently use similar tactics myself. What went around came around and if you did a good job u never had any problems. But a dealer would have to earn the pit's respect first.

Locals played a crucial role in making markets when Liffe first opened. As dealers depended on the success of these markets for their livelihood, it was not in their interests to always try to rip off the market makers. I also did not want to see my friends lose money. I got plenty of business and trades on the floor which I can attribute in part to my reputation for being an honest dealer. In fact, in the early days the vast majority of traders never did anything that would bring the market into disrepute. Brokers and traders alike all wanted the exchange to be a success and we were prepared to help each other out in a way which may not always have been by the book but was never unethical. A slight bending of the rules actually had the effect of benefiting the market in the long run as it made for a more efficient market. After all, we were all paying £2,000 a month to lease a seat so we felt entitled to try and get an edge here and there.

While the Liffe floor at the Royal Exchange had its fair share of dealers bending the rules and using bullying tactics to make money it was a somewhat gentrified place compared with the bear pits across the other side of the Atlantic in Chicago. Kevin Thomas, a Liffe trader whose moustache and glasses had earned him the nickname Identikit Man, found out first hand just how tough dealing in the CME could be. As the Eurodollar contract is traded in both London and Chicago, Thomas became a member of the CME and after visiting brokers he did business with in Chicago he decided to put his membership to use and spend a week trading on the floor. Being confident and ambitious, he had worked on the theory that if he wanted to be a top Eurodollar trader Chicago was the place he had to be.

On Monday morning he strolled on to a heaving CME floor wearing a badge emblazoned with the words 'new member'. It might as well have read 'fresh meat'. As he walked past the S&P 500 options pit a broker spotted his badge and scribbled down an out trade in his name. The next morning a clerk would ask Thomas if he had been dealing in the S&P 500 options. Thomas looked baffled. After the clerk retraced his steps and found out that Thomas has walked past the pit he soon realised that the Londoner had been the victim of one of the oldest tricks on the exchange floor. Luckily for Thomas, he was not held to the trade. The S&P index frequently had massive spikes in volatility. Having an erroneous out trade to your name could cost you thousands of dollars. Thomas would later notice that dealers covered their badges when walking near this part of the exchange. This was dog-eat-dog stuff and not at all British.

Thomas could handle the rough and tumble on the Liffe floor. But he felt dwarfed by the dealers at the CME. He said that they all looked about seven feet tall! Many were former American football players and basketball players who had not been good enough to make the cut. Dealers walked into the pits half an hour before trading started with their hands raised high. The pits were so crammed full it would be almost impossible for a trader to lift their arms up once inside the pits and their feet could often be lifted off the ground in the melee. The heat from the crowded floor was intense and Thomas recalled being soaked in sweat after just 10 minutes. Fortunately he had taken care of the all the calls of nature beforehand. Once dealing started there would be no escape until trading finished six and a half hours later. Thomas would later hear stories of dealers p**sing themselves on the floor rather than leave their spot while trading big positions.

When Thomas got to work in the Eurodollar pit he started bidding and offering with the best off them but nobody would trade with him. Everyone nearby was getting business but not him. After his first day, the only trade he had to his name was the phantom out trade from the S&P 500 options pit. He could not fathom why everybody was ignoring him. The next day he decided to give up the edge (which locals hate doing) and hit the bid or lift the offer so that he could get a trade off. He walked up to the biggest broker nearby (both physically and business wise) and yelled 'Buy 20'. The broker just blanked him. 'Didn't you hear me? Buy 20,' repeated Thomas. This time he got a response. 'F**k off, you've done nothing,' said the dealer.

It was left to another trader to explain why nobody would trade with him. It was quite simple. He was not one of them and nobody wanted to risk having an out trade with the new boy. The next day, Thomas went up to the same broker and yelled: 'Buy 100 at six and sell you 100 at five.' This handed the broker a $2,500 gift. Thomas then made similar trades with some of the other brokers nearby. These trades functioned as an entrance fee and people started to trade with him from then onwards. He was never ignored again. Joining the club had cost him more than $5,000. Now he had the privilege of being treated like dirt in the same way as the thousands of other dealers working on the floor. Later in the week, Thomas found himself among a group of locals that were feeding orders off one portly broker. The intense heat from the floor made the slobbering broker sweat profusely. Every so often he would wipe his brow with a trading card and flick droplets of sweat on to the locals who were circling him. Thomas thought this gesture summed up what the broker thought of the locals he worked with every day.

The vast expanse of the CME floor meant that dealers could only trade single months which were separated into different zones by white dividing lines scrawled on to the floor. In London dealers could trade all the individual months of a contract from one spot. The size of the CME floor meant that if a dealer wanted to trade a spread he would need to be able to move from one section of the floor to another. This was impossible given how cramped the floor was and sometimes two dealers would work as a team and trade with each other between different sections of the pit. Thomas had not realised this when he started dealing which made him make the mistake of accepting a spread trade, in which one month is purchased and another sold. As the other month was traded on another side of the pit he had no way of getting out of the position. Thomas was trapped with an open position which left his financial wellbeing in the hands of the Gods. He had to wait until trading closed on the floor before dashing to call his broker to close the position – by which time a winning trade had turned into a losing one.

Thomas would never trade in the CME pits again. His experiences reminded me of tennis match that took place in *Money*, a novel written by the English writer Martin Amis. The main protagonist in the novel, an advertising executive named John Self, agreed to play his American business partner Fielding Goodney at an exclusive New

York City tennis club. While the slobbering Self was a run-of-the-mill grass court player in England he found himself no match for his American foe who systematically drove him into the ground, smashing in serves and volleys like a player on the professional tennis circuit. Amis said he used the match to illustrate the differences between America, which his character Self described as 'a vigorous mongrel', and the 'blasted, totalled, broken-winded, shot-faced London, doing time under sodden skies.' While dealing on Liffe's Cannon Bridge floor in later years would become every bit as ferociously competitive as the Chicago pits, an English gentleman could certainly have a torrid time on the other side of the Atlantic. One London trader turned up at the CME to trade the S&P 500 index dressed in an immaculate three-piece, pinstripe suit while wearing spotless well-polished black shoes. His smart attire did not go unnoticed on an exchange floor where wearing a tie wrapped around your waist was enough to meet the dress code requirements. Needless to say his brightly polished black shoes were well trodden on before the day's trading was done.

Locals on the Liffe floor could be just as vulnerable to cannons firing financial bombs out of America as the rest of the world's economies when the excesses of US capitalism come unstuck. John Meriwether was in his prime as head of the domestic fixed income arbitrage group at Salomon Brothers when the Liffe market started to take off in the early eighties. Meriwether would often call dealers at Liffe to execute trades for him. During his tenure as Salomon's floor manager in London, Ersser regularly spoke to Meriwether. The pair shared a love of horse racing and would often talk about their interest in the sport. On one occasion, Elliot Carling, who worked for Meriwether, started selling short sterling down. After the market had fallen 30 ticks a broker representing a consortium of UK clearing banks approached Ersser and told him they would buy the balance of his order. When Ersser informed Elliot of this he was told "be gentle with them, just say they really don't want to buy anymore". Salomon continued to sell and eventually forced the Bank of England to raise interest rates. Ersser once got a call from Meriwether himself.

'Where is short sterling Teddy?' he asked.

'They are 19 bid at 20,' replied Ersser.

'Teddy they should be trading 50. I want to see them trading 50 by the time New York opens. Get to work!' ordered Meriwether.

'Sorry John are you asking me to buy everything up to 50?' was Ersser's fuddled 'English' reply.

'YES. Only call me when you have reached the price or bought more than 50 thousand lots,' demanded Meriwether before slamming the telephone down.

This was a massive order. Any local unlucky enough to have sold at 20 was definitely in for a bad time and could end up on their way to filing for bankruptcy before the day was over. Seeing these types of orders explode into the market kept you sharp. One lapse of concentration could result in you losing everything. Bruce Kovner, who was one of the world's largest traders in the interbank currency and futures market during his tenure at Commodities Corporation, felt that traders who tried to push the market up or down with massive buy or sell orders were doomed to fail themselves one day. 'It can be done in the short-term. But eventually it will lead to serious mistakes. It usually results in arrogance and a loss of touch with the underlying market structure, both technically and structurally,' said Kovner in an interview in the late eighties. Meriwether went on to found the Greenwich, Connecticut-based Long Term Capital Management (LTCM) in 1994. The hedge fund commanded more than $100 billion in assets at its peak. But LTCM's bets on the financial market in the late nineties would blow up spectacularly – resulting in $4.6 billion of losses in less than four months after the Russian financial crisis – and almost bring down the entire global financial system.

5

The Royal Exchange Days

Not everyone in the City may have wanted to see Liffe become a permanent part of life in the square mile. But to dealers like myself, the exchange was the promised land. We were tremendously determined to make it a success. As my own career took off I enjoyed watching dealing volumes at the Royal Exchange soar. Those who doubted that England had the right capitalist atmosphere to support a major futures exchange had underestimated what a bunch of East End and South London boys could do when let loose in such a meritocratic environment. The barman at The Greenhouse soon got used to Liffe traders walking into the bar and ordering 'Two bottles of your best shampoo mate.' Business was good and we were all hungry for more.

Liffe recorded its first million traded contracts on 5 August 1983. This figure soon doubled to two million on 9 March 1984. By this time, the average dealing volume ran at 10,220, almost double the 1983 average of 5,400. What the hell it was we were doing inside the Royal Exchange was still a mystery to most people though. Whenever anybody asked me what I did for a living I would refer to the movie *Trading Places*. In the eighties box office smash hit film,

Philadelphia executive Louis Winthorpe III (played by Dan Aykroyd) 'trades places' with ghetto-man Billy Ray Valentine (played by Eddie Murphy). I thought the film did a great job of conjuring up the madness of the trading floor with dealers shouting buy and sell orders into each other's faces.

I had been elected on to the pit and floor committees in 1987. This made me responsible for supervising the behaviour of traders on the floor, dealing with disciplinary incidents and sitting on the panel responsible for trading exams. A right of passage for young aspiring traders were the pit exams. Trading exams were a bit of a joke when the exchange first opened and the knowledge some dealers had about the financial instruments which they traded was not always encyclo-paedic. When Doris took part in an ITV documentary on the Liffe floor he was asked by the interviewer what a financial future was to which he answered 'You'll have to cut this. There's a good answer but I don't know it.' Nevertheless, the tests did become increasingly rigorous as Liffe established itself at the Royal Exchange. Most trainee traders had served their apprenticeship as yellow-jacketed runners or clerks. The pit exam could make or break many a promising career. Candidates had to pass a series of written exams on the futures and options market. But the real test took place in mock trading sessions. These were conducted in the evening after dealing on the exchange floor had finished. About 20 prospective traders would assemble on the Liffe floor and wait to be tested. Here they stood wooden-faced, nervously waiting for the bell to ring to commence trading. The mock dealing exams would be an exceptionally nerve-racking experience for new recruits. Many would be visibly trembling during and after the test. Trainees would be assessed on the accuracy of their trades after being given a series of orders which had to be filled. Prospective dealers would have to be able to spot the bid and offer prices coming into the market and prove that they knew what they were doing when executing trades. To be successful, a candidate would need to be mentally quick to digest the orders being fired into the market while also being tough enough to hold their own on the floor. The physical nature of the trading pits meant that those who shrank into their shell were not going to go far. To make the mock exercises as real as possible, experienced dealers would join trainees in the pits and move the market up and down, simulating the market conditions of an interest rate hike or stock market crash. Being adept at using the right hand signals to execute trades was a crucial skill. Trainees would spend hours practising their hand gestures in front of the mirror in preparation for their exam. One dealer earned the nickname Cabbage after he admitted practising the hand movements in the vegetable plot at the end of his garden while his wife watched to make sure he got the signals right.

When the mock exercise had finished, the examiners would mark each candidate's dealing card to check if it had been completed correctly. The number of errant out trades would also be recorded. I would regularly mark these pit exams as part of my role as a member of the pit and floor committees before overseeing the interview. The Liffe staff would provide myself and a couple of assistants with the results of the written and pit tests but it was up to us to decide if a candidate had passed or failed. The decision could be life-changing for many and it was highly rewarding work when an elated candidate passed. Failing people was not that much fun though. While I struggle to remember those I assessed, every trader would remember the people that gave them a chance to deal on the floor. Success would mean becoming a trainee blue button, which would double a candidate's salary overnight. Failure would not just severely dent a trainee's career aspirations in the City. It would also mean being excluded from a social scene which he or she desperately wanted to be a part of. Those who did not make the cut would be left spending their working days attending to humdrum administrative tasks as runners or clerks while their mates moved on to the floor to try and earn their stripes alongside the star traders.

As my own career developed at the Royal Exchange I also took part in supervising blue buttons starting out on the market. I have enjoyed coaching traders throughout my career. My passion for the job always shines through which usually boosts a trainee's enthusiasm to learn the trade. New traders would need all the help that they could get. Like sharks smelling blood, more experienced dealers would put them under pressure as much as they could. Trainees would ask for help in trading spreads and I would show them what to do and then make sure that they traded what was known as the value trade or good leg with me. The trainees would be happy that their orders were filled without any errors while I would obtain a trading edge. Working with blue buttons also helped me spot the new talent coming on to the floor which could make promising new recruits for Morgan Sussex.

There was no magic template for what made a successful trader. A hunger and strong desire to do the job were the mandatory requirements as was a good aptitude for mental arithmetic. Many of the trainees who failed just did not have a strong enough personality or the mental quickness needed to read orders properly. Some may have been Oxbridge-educated and fluent in four languages, but would find themselves at a loss when trying to summon the mental aptitude needed to do the job of an order filler. While most successful locals were working class, being from a privileged elite background was not a barrier to making it as a trader and the dealing floor became a bit of a melting pot. Former building site workers and sons of market stall traders would rub shoulders with university graduates. Lord Daniel Beckett, whose mother was a lady in waiting to the Queen Mother, carved out a career as a trader.

Terry Crawley's success on the floor earned him millions and made him one of the most successful London locals of all time. His story illustrated just how accessible the Liffe floor was. When he was taking part in the pit exams, someone had asked who he used to work for. 'Allied mate, he used to work for Allied,' replied a trainee.

'What, Allied Irish Banks?' asked the other fellow.
'No. Allied Carpets,' was the reply.

The little technology that was used to support dealing on the Royal Exchange floor seems very primitive indeed these days. If a broker made a mistake on an order, tape-recorded telephone conversations were used to apportion blame in the disputed transaction. Cargill Investor Services, the UK-based broking subsidiary of the American giant Cargill, was involved in such a dispute when it purchased the wrong contract for a client, resulting in a massive trading loss. The senior management from Cargill came down to the floor to listen to the tapes for themselves. This was serious stuff! Dogsy, the order filler and telephone broker involved in the dispute, was also required to be present when the tapes were played. He was mindful that a dealer could lose his job if he was found to be responsible for a serious error, which could cost his company thousands of pounds. A deafening silence ensued as the tapes were played covering the few minutes before the disputed trade had taken place. A room full of exchange staff and senior brokers listened in. Suddenly the words of a familiar voice rang out.

'Can I have £40 to win on the next race?' asked Dogsy.
'Do you want to stay on the line for the commentary?' asked his bookkeeper.
'Of course!' he answered.

Dogsy was left to listen to the horserace that he had a bet on before the disputed transaction while wishing the ground would swallow him up there and then. Several minutes later the customer came on to the line and the exchange was able to settle the disputed trade. Luckily for Dogsy, it turned out that he had not been at fault so he did not have to face any penalties. But he knew that his recorded racing punt would never be forgotten!

The biggest scandal on the floor of the Royal Exchange involved five member firms being fined and nine traders being suspended from the exchange after being implicated in a tax evasion and money laundering scam. An unscrupulous broker received a one-year suspension from the exchange. The penalties were handed down by the exchange after an eight-month investigation which was concluded in August 1987. The scam involved a variety of different schemes set up to move trading profits to the offshore island of Jersey through pre-arranged trades executed outside the pits. Wads of cash were then stashed into suitcases and bought back into the country from Jersey.

The Royal Exchange floor was certainly not free of unethical behaviour but there were far more murky places to be found in the

City of London at that time. One broker assumed the role of a pillar of society with his 'support' for an old aged pensioners' home. When the Conservative government privatised a major nationalised industry – in its bid to promote widespread share ownership among the British public – he persuaded 50 residents of the home to apply for shares using his funds. After the shares were floated on the stock exchange and dutifully jumped up in value he took a quick profit on the stocks which he had assumed ownership of, netting a profit of tens of thousands of pounds. The grateful pensioners were happily rewarded with a new colour television.

In the summer of 1987 the exchange celebrated its fifth anniversary, the highlight of which was a floor party held on a Friday night. Rik Mayall, who was the star of the cult comedy series *The Young Ones*, had the job of entertaining a floor packed full of traders. A temporary stage was constructed on the dealing floor and pretty waitresses served thirsty traders with glasses of champagne. We were entertained by a cabaret act first before Rik Mayall took to the stage dressed in a trading jacket while assuming the obnoxious demeanour of his *Young Ones* character. He thought it would be fun to take the mickey out of all of us. This was a big mistake! While we could laugh at ourselves he crossed the line and it was not long before he was getting heckled with chants of 'who are ya, who are ya?' Trading cards were thrown at him like confetti. One card hit him right between the eyes. But he gamely continued his act, calling us all 'w*****s' and sticking two fingers up as dealing cards rained down on him. It must have been the toughest gig of his life! John Wells, who was performing his famous Denis Thatcher impersonation, was so horrified at the way Mayall had been treated that he refused to go on stage afterwards. Eventually he was persuaded to make an appearance. But he cut his half-hour act down to a four-minute slot.

6

Local Heroes

Alan Dickinson was glowing as we sank a few glasses of champagne one Friday afternoon at The Greenhouse. He had a broad smile to match his bristly dark brown moustache as he told me about a big position that he had taken in the Bund options market. He was sitting on a profit of £983,000 but he was not going to take a profit until the trade hit the top of the market. In his opinion, this would be when the Bund reached a price that would make him £1 million. He refused to be spoofed by any price fluctuations. This open position could go up and down like a whore's drawers – no matter if it gyrated from a profit of £456,000, dropped to £60,000 before moving back up to £675,000 – £1 million is what it had to be.

When I spoke to Dickinson a couple of weeks later about the trade he was not in quite such good form. He confided that the market had reached its peak soon after we last spoke about the trade and he had ended up scratching the position to make a paltry profit of a few thousand pounds. Most dealers would have snatched at a profit on that trade when it had reached £10,000. But Dickinson was a trader who never flinched from following his convictions on what trades to make. It just so happened that this time his antenna had not quite been in tune with where the market was heading. The fact that this had cost him almost £1 million was not something he was going to lose any sleep over. Neither would his confidence in being able to predict the market be dented. It just so happened he had been wrong this time and he took it like a man and just laughed about it. Easy come easy go!

When the exchange opened in 1982 there were only a handful of pure local traders. Dickinson was the best and most well known. Like me, he was inspired to be a trader in London after seeing how futures and options were traded across the other side of the Atlantic. He had worked as a dealer in the commodities markets in New York before the Liffe market opened and he put down his family savings of £15,000 and borrowed £30,000 to buy a seat on the exchange. Mentally and physically tough with a quick mind and supreme belief in his abilities, Dickinson was a trailblazer among the new breed of London traders stalking the Liffe floor. He allegedly became the first millionaire at Liffe and his success would be an inspiration to traders starting out on the floor like myself. He went on to sponsor other traders and extract a percentage of their profits as part of his AJD Futures venture. By the mid-nineties there were about 800 locals on the exchange floor following in Dickinson's footsteps.

Locals were the life blood of the Liffe market. Rather than working for a bank or following the instructions of a customer, locals traded on their own account. A trader was classified as a local if he took on the risk of at least 50% of his trading profits or losses. Thousands of pounds could be made – or lost – in a single day's trading. Dealing with such high stakes on a daily basis made locals by far the best traders on the floor. I am certain that the Liffe market would not have been able to succeed were it not for the contribution which locals made in the early days of the exchange. While the local community grew in size as the Liffe market became more established, there was only ever an elite band of people which could count themselves as being a cut above the rest. The herd mentality ruled the dealing decisions of most locals who would join the fray in buying or selling whatever was on the move.

Opening Bell day one. A polite 'excuse me' will get you nowhere in this crowd.

Eurodollar pit, 1984.

Royal Exchange floor.

Day one Traders.

Royal Visit, 1991.

Meeting Prince Philip, Royal Visit, 1991.

BTP pit.

The Cannon Bridge trading floor.

SXL staff football team playing at Upton Park, Back row left to right: Dean Sheppard (runner), Russell Kean (FTSE), David 'Macca' Roser (BTP), Steve Colderwood (ECU), John, Peter Moffat (Eurolira), Nigel 'Mad Dog' Bewick. Front row left to right: Ben Farrier (runner), Michael Debenham (runner), Scott Johnson (Eurolira), Clive Beauchamp (ECU), Paul Wood (head runner).

Liffe old boys playing at Wembley stadium. Back row: Alan Dickinson third from the left; Keith Penny back right. Front row: John third from right; Clive Beauchamp second from right.

The Omen, Spencer winning the European title sponsored by Sussex Futures.

Some of the old boys at John's retirement evening left to right: Simon 'Milky' Blackburn, Mark Wager, Clive Beauchamp, Nigel Ackerman, Kevin Thomas, John, Bubble, Keith Penny, Macca, Darren Chesterton, Grant 'Gurner' Maton.

The vast majority of dealers were salaried traders when the market first opened. Notable exceptions included LaPorta and his fellow American Mark Stanton at Smith Brothers, the London-based market maker. These guys initially never owned seats or deposited their own money. They just traded the market and took a share of the profits. When the exchange first opened there were others like myself who had trading accounts but chose to work for companies. This meant that we did not risk our own money and took a salary for filling an employer's orders. The best we could hope for if trading went well would be a better bonus on the back of any profits that we earned. Traders like me soon realised that we could make much more by dealing for ourselves rather than just making an employer rich. Gather enough cash to lease a seat and place a deposit with a clearing company and you were free to play the market on your own. This type of entrepreneurial spirit epitomised what populist Thatcherism was all about. No wonder some scribes in the popular press started calling us Maggie's boys!

Each local had his own style. I had a very consistent approach in my dealing strategy and always looked for value. I never took unnecessary risks and had a hard work ethic. There was always a plan and a structure. If a trade did not work out, a position would be closed immediately before I looked for the next opportunity. 'Hope' never came into the equation. A famous saying on the floor was that there were two hopes – Bob and no hope. And Bob had just left town. Trading and gambling may be poles apart but the best professional gamblers often have a similar strategy to the tactics I used in the pits – looking for a consistent and steady return from their efforts rather than risking everything on a big win. You will not see a top professional gambler walking into a casino and wagering everything he owns on red at the roulette table. Being risk averse was a good characteristic to have if you wanted a career on the floor which would last.

Many locals were highly skilled order fillers who executed floor brokerage for other member firms at the exchange and occasionally traded on their own account when a good opportunity emerged. The biggest risk which these guys faced was out trades. One of the best order fillers in the market in the early days was Andy Martin, a trader who filled paper for Salomon Brothers in the Eurodollar pit. Whenever a broker came into the pit and messed up an order – which could involve buying the wrong month or quantity, missing the trade altogether or just failing to get a fair price – he would always say 'pay peanuts get monkeys'. There was a lot of truth to this saying. A quality order filler would save his firm a fortune. Dealers that were not up to the job were a danger to themselves and those around them. There was no point in paying an order filler £20,000 a year if his out trades were costing hundreds of thousands of pounds. I would get annoyed when I heard an embittered banker talk about how rankled he got at the sight of a young dealer from Liffe driving an Aston Martin. The fact was 99% of these traders deserved the money that they were making and the banker himself would probably not have lasted five minutes in the pits.

Locals that sought to profit from very small price fluctuations were known as pure scalpers. Dealers needed a lightning quick mind to do this job well. A scalper would attempt to profit from the edge available in buying at the bid price and quickly selling at the offered price. This was a low risk, high frequency strategy which generated a regular profit stream and also provided liquidity in the market. This trading style contrasted with the more technical chartist approach, which involved using charts which displayed historical trading data. Price charts were used by a dealer in an effort to find patterns that in the past preceded falling or rising prices. When the development of similar patterns emerged in the current market traders guided by charts interpreted this as a signal of a probable market move in the same direction. Data tools would be scrutinised for breakout points – price movements beyond a previous high (or low) or outside the boundaries of a preceding price consolidation – which would allow a dealer to run a position for several ticks. If the market traded up and produced a buy signal a dealer would buy and run it.

Arbitrage became a popular technique used by many dealers on the floor. In essence, arbitrage involves buying a futures contract at a cheap price in one market while simultaneously selling at a higher price in another. The profit margins on this strategy are small so arbitrageurs deal in large volumes to generate a good income. The most infamous arbitrager of them all was Nick Leeson. He was supposed to be using arbitrage to profit from differences in the prices of the Nikkei-225 futures contracts listed on the Osaka Securities Exchange in Japan and SIMEX in Singapore. Of course, his dealing strategies veered somewhat from being low risk. Spread traders would try to get an edge by trading two contract months at the same time – buying one and selling the other – before possibly buying back the short month to run a long position.

Dickinson's rival for the title of king of the pits in the early days was Nigel Ackerman, who almost assumed the role of elder statesman of the dealing room floor. Ackerman already had a sprinkling of grey hair to match a neatly trimmed bushy mustache which gave him a Cheshire cat like grin when he smiled. Standing over six feet tall, Ackerman had a natural presence in the pit, having already honed his trading skills before the exchange opened while serving as a spread trader in the commodities markets. While many dealers would try to copy how the green-jacketed Ackerman went about the task of jobbing the market, few would succeed. He had an exceptionally quick analytical mind which enabled him to quickly read – and take advantage of – price movements even in extreme market conditions. Ackerman understood all the complicated trading strategies better than anyone else, which enabled him to make prices in any spread. When people first started to contemplate the move to screen-based trading there was a consensus among dealers at the time that it would be impossible for a machine to replicate what Ackerman could do. He had an intuitive understanding of value. This enabled him to hedge large positions using sophisticated spreading strategies to reduce his exposure to financial risks in the market. This meant he was never scared to trade large-size positions, which could consist of several thousand lots of futures contracts with a market value of half a billion pounds.

Ackerman allegedly became the first man on the commodity markets to negotiate a guaranteed percentage profit share from the commodity trading firm that he worked for. When the Liffe floor opened, word of his success soon got out and he was asked to take part in a television documentary about the exchange in the early eighties. Viewers saw him enjoying all the trappings of success, including the big house, swimming pool, Rolls Royce and racing horses. Ackerman took a bit of stick from the lads on the floor after the documentary. But the money and success never changed him and he tried to make sure that the rest of us kept our feet firmly on the ground. If any of the young upstarts on the floor ever stepped out of line he would put them in their place. One word from Ackerman was enough to shut any one of them up. He had a really dry sense of humour and would give other dealers his own personalised nick-names. When Llama (Andy Hughes) walked past his pit he would say 'Hello Curly'. The fact that everyone else called him Lama did not matter to Ackerman. He had a knack for making quips of one or two words which came almost out of the side of his mouth. If a woman walked past the pit he would say Anita before pausing and uttering the word Harris, which was slang for arse. Anita Harris was a female singer in the early seventies and only a handful of traders had any idea what he was going on about.

David Kyte began his career as a local in January 1985 with the help of family money. The North London man had already proved his abilities on the floor with successful stints at Comfin, the commodity broker, and Tulletts. I first met him in the pit practice sessions that Alex Lamb ran at Comfin. He was a couple of years younger than me and had joined from a stock broker. It was clear right away that Kyte had a great enthusiasm for trading. He tore into the practice sessions with gusto, enjoying every second. He epitomised the hungry dealer in a hurry to get to the very top. When the market opened he made sure that he was learning about the business faster than every-one else. He would often come over to my booth in the morning and ask how to calculate the forward forwards in the cash market. He would also ask for my opinion on where I expected the market to open. He would soak up the information which I gave him like a sponge. After a while he stopped coming round. I think he had learned all he needed from me and had moved on.

Kyte was a great spread trader who also took positions in the market. Sometimes he would come into my pit and ask what was there. I would make a price that I would be happy to trade on with anybody else but if he hit my bid or lifted my offer I would immediately feel that I had made a mistake – I never saw him take a loss. He seemed invincible. Years later I discovered that if he ever accumulated losses he would get a broker to close out his position. When he made a profit on the other hand he would close the positions out himself. Like other successful dealers, he understood the importance of assuming the aura of invincibility. Only dealers blessed with a sixth sense – like Terry Crawley – could detect when Kyte was in trouble on the floor. Crawley said Kyte had a nervous tic which was particularly transparent to him, not that I – or I am pretty damn sure anyone else on the floor – could see it.

Kyte once took on Goldman Sachs, the US investment bank. 'What are you doing taking on Goldman?' I asked. I would only take a position against a major bank if I knew that it was just hedging its own risks – rather than taking an outright position in the markets. Banks such as ANZ Bank, BNP Paribas and Hambros would be safe to deal with as I knew their dealers were just covering risks in other markets. Goldman Sachs was another story! Kyte was unfazed though. 'Goldman Sachs. Big deal. At the end of the day I am just trading against another man. He just happens to work for a big bank. I bet you he is more worried than me right now. Because I know that I am right,' he said. 'If he wants to buy more I will sell him more!' He had the courage and self-confidence to back his judgement with the underlying belief that he was the superior trader. He would say that the reason he liked trading so much was that it allowed him to go it alone and be in command of his own destiny. Kyte went on to set up The Kyte Group in 1985, which has grown into a highly successful trading and clearing group based in North London. He once said that working for himself was 'the ultimate meritocracy', which meant that he was worth exactly what he made, no more, no less. Kyte was a multi-millionaire when I last looked at the *Sunday Times Rich List*. But like some other exceptionally gifted traders, he has not lost his love for the business. Rather than spending his days on a yacht in the South of France, Kyte still works full-time as a trader, pursuing complex dealing strategies across a plethora of financial markets. This means starting work at 6:45 every morning to trade 13-hour days at his desk.

The traders with the biggest balls in the pits had a trading style which resembled that of a world class poker player. A sixth sense on where the market was heading would guide their dealing strategies. This was as close to gambling as trading can get. Once they had a hunch for where the market was heading they would position themselves so a broker on the other end of a trade could be squeezed as much as possible. Like a world class gambler at a card table in a casino, they had the skill of being able to look a broker in the eye and read if he had a big order, a stop or a market order. This sixth sense would give them the intuition to know who was short and long in the market. It was incredible to watch these guys at work. Not only would they be trading on instinct but they would have the balls of steel needed to take on the big banks, dealing in thousands of lots of contracts at a single time. Markets would move and a six-figure profit could be regularly made in just one day.

Terry Crawley was an exponent of the art of intuitive trading. To the untrained eye, Crawley may have appeared as little more than a bully, swaggering around the pit like a giant in his own kingdom. He once said: 'This is my world and you lot just live in it.' This comment was a lot more about cultivating an intimidating image, rather than being the words of a genuinely arrogant man. Being successful in the pits was a tough game and Crawley was a master at being able to play it. He would intimidate other traders to trade with him on his terms. But there was nothing particularly menacing about Crawley's demeanour. Smartly combed short dark brown hair and a medium build and height certainly did not give him an intimidating appearance. Beneath a braggadocio front was a man with an acute understanding of the fundamentals of the market, using basic dealing techniques to reap massive rewards.

The Sun newspaper famously did a front page story about Crawley's 'rugs to riches' story, which revealed how the former carpet fitter had made nearly £10 million trading financial futures in one year. But there was nothing lucky about the way he got to the top. Crawley developed his own system of trading in which the market would be broken down from one year, to one month, to one week, to one day, to one minute. He was even conscious that there was a market within a market. But the fundamental question always remained the same. What is the value of the trade? He had the value of every trade which he executed preprogrammed in his mind.

Crawley would start his working day by chatting to the women who worked in the booth at JP Morgan to pick their brains on where the markets were due to open. He would look to see how the markets in South East Asia had traded over night and where the US investment bank's dealers thought the BTP pit was going to open from the previous night's close. He would also have scanned the Reuters news feed and leafed through the day's *Financial Times*, though he would say the paper looked like yesterday's racing results, reporting on events which had already taken place. When the market opened, Crawley would watch closely how other dealers in the pit reacted, while keeping his mind on what he thought the true value was. His own dealing strategy would then be executed when he could see exactly what was happening around him. As the day progressed he would look at the flows coming into the market and how other traders responded to the events of the day. The BTP pit was exceptionally volatile which enabled him to exert his own influence on where prices were heading.

Unlike most of the locals on the floor who were following the herd, Crawley would always have the balls to follow his own convictions, even if it meant trading against other locals on occasions, which meant making money at their expense. This did not always make him the most popular man in the pits. On more than one occasion an envious floor trader would get tanked up at lunch time and come back on to the floor looking to have a punch up with Crawley. Even some of the pit officials – who had the job of ensuring an orderly well-behaved market – wanted to see the 'arrogant' Crawley take a few punches which meant that he did not always get the protection that he needed when a thug tried to take a pop at him. Crawley was always too smart to get into a fight though he was once hauled in front of the exchange's disciplinary panel for verbally abusing a senior pit official, who was known as Moose. The pair had got into an argument over the reporting of some trades. Crawley was adamant that a trade he had made was good. But Moose refused to let the trade stand. Crawley responded to this by calling Moose a c**t. The incident was then reported. When questioned by the panel Crawley again called Moose a c**t and was handed a fine. Crawley then asked the panel: 'What if I only think he's a c**t?'

'You can think whatever you like,' replied a member of the panel. 'Good, because I think he's a c**t,' retorted Crawley.

Being the top boy in the pits was certainly no easy place to be. But when he retired, Crawley would be able to boast that in all his years at the exchange he never once got beat (lost money). He would also walk away from the Liffe market when the floor closed with an alleged £30 million fortune in the bank.

LaPorta traded in a similar vein to Crawley. He also had the incredible ability to look a broker in the eye and make a split-second judgement on what type of order the dealer had. LaPorta would then act on whatever his gut instinct was telling him. He had the courage to sit on what looked like losing positions which would very often turn around before pouncing to make a tidy profit. Other dealers would say that LaPorta's booming Chicagoan voice alone could move markets! He arrived in London at the age of 26, being among the band of Chicago dealers who crossed the pond to make some easy money in London when the Liffe market first opened. But unlike others who left when dealing got competitive, LaPorta stayed. His success on the floor had made him a millionaire in the mid-eighties and a 'double-millionaire' in 1994. But his lack of discipline meant that he never achieved the riches of other Local heroes. 'Making the money is the easy part. Keeping it is the game,' he would later lament. 'I was a party animal numbing myself on a daily basis. When a person numbs themselves on a daily basis they make bad decisions. Not only did my addictive personality cost me a lot of money it also cost me a marriage.'

If Dickinson was the original king of the pit, Mark Green would be the first young contender to have a legitimate claim for taking his crown. Green quickly became the number one trader in the Eurodollar pit, upsetting a good many traders on the way. He was certainly more feared than loved. But while there were many traders who did not like him, there were few who did not respect Green. He had big *cojones* and would routinely take on massive positions. He would force brokers to trade with him at his price.

Green was able to routinely take huge positions in the market because he was backed by Roger Carlsson, who owned First Continental Trading (FCT), the clearing company. Carlsson, a native of Sweden, was in his forties at the time and had balding hair and a bit of a paunch. He was a shrewd businessman who had made his millions in the options business in Chicago. He had subsequently opened offices in London, Milan and Singapore. Carlsson was one of the richest men in the market. In 1988 he increased Green's dealing limits from 200 lots to 500 lots. This was 10 times the limit I imposed on myself and probably bigger than the limits of any other local at that time. The underlying value of each lot was $1 million, which was quite a lot of money in the eighties.

Green was never afraid to use the privileges awarded to him by his paymaster. He even broke his own expansive dealing limits in one trade which made him the first local to take on a position with a value of more than $1 billion. This enabled him to make a quick $28,550 profit in less than half a minute. When he phoned Carlsson in Chicago to give an explanation of what happened he got a b******ing. But not for the reasons he had expected. 'You got me out of the pit to tell me that [you broke your trading limits],' yelled Carlsson. 'That is why I employ you. To take the risks and make money!'

Green's risk taking on the floor did not always result in winning trades. In 1992 he built up a huge short position (when a dealer bets on prices falling) of 2,000 lots in London while the markets waited for the US unemployment figure to be released on the Friday afternoon. The economic figure was set to be announced a couple of minutes after the dealing pits in Chicago opened. Green could not risk running the whole position into the number so he gave an order to buy 1,000 lots in Chicago just before it was released. The data was very bullish and within seconds it was 40 ticks higher. Green was forced to bite the bullet and buy the other 1,000 lots in Chicago, netting a $1 million loss. This turned out to be what traders describe as a 'good cut'. The market rallied another 20 ticks, which would have cost Green another half a million dollars. The traders in Chicago thought Green was God! These dealers had seen him buy 1,000 lots before the number was released and saw him buy another 1,000 lots 40 ticks higher, before it leapt up another 20 ticks. It looked like he had just made a quick $2 million. The pit traders in Chicago had no idea that Green was only covering a short position that he had in London. This meant that in reality he had lost $1 million. Green had no inclination to reveal the true story. He would let them believe what they liked. Green left the exchange that evening in a downbeat mood without going to the pub. Being able to cope with a big loss is an important part of being a successful trader. Green would reflect that his mind had not been properly focused on trading when he made the losing trade. He had recently lost his father to cancer and had perhaps returned back to the market too soon. Having lost his mother as a young child, Green's father had been a rock of support when he was growing up. When Green returned to work on Monday morning he was determined to quickly make back the money that he had lost. The shock of a $1 million dollar loss had been enough to restore his razor sharp focus. Within a month he had succeeded in making the whole million dollars back.

Green never backed down from the opportunity to make a winning trade. In 1996 David Helps, a senior broker at JP Morgan, told him that their cash desk was prepared to pay a particular price for 10,000 Euromark contracts even though the market was trading a few ticks lower. Helps asked Green if he could sell all these contracts. JP Morgan was prepared to pay a small premium to get the whole order completed in one ticket. This was by far the biggest trade any local had ever done on the floor and although it would give Green a huge edge it also exposed him to an equally huge risk. He had enemies trading for the big banks who were just waiting to punish him if he ever overextended himself in the market. Nevertheless Green agreed to do the trade. He regularly took on huge positions for relatively small rewards. 'It was never about ego, the size of the trade meant f**k all to me. It was all just about making money,' he once said.

Tremendous self-belief gave him a sense of certainty as to whe
true value of the market was. He hedged the massive position in other
markets while covering as many Euromarks as he could. His cool
calculated mind enabled him to profit from a transaction no other
local would have even dared take on.

Not everyone appreciated Green's style. He locked horns with a
lot of dealers but the most long-running feud took place between him
and Ersser, when he was the floor manager at Salomon Brothers.
Ersser's greying hair by this time had earned him the nickname
Badger. He was the most powerful man on the floor. Things had to
be done just one way – his way. The mighty Salomon gave all their
business out to locals and Ersser had the job of deciding who got
what. This meant that everybody wanted to be his friend. Ersser was
not used to being shown no respect by a dealer half his age. This is
what he had to eat up from Green every day. Neither guy was going
to back down or show the other any respect. Consequently, turf war
erupted in the Eurodollar pit as Green routinely took on Ersser and
the full might of Salomon. He wasn't afraid of anyone.

The eighties may have just come to an end but Salomon was still
the undisputed king in the Eurodollar pit. You could almost see the
cogs going round in Ersser's mind when he watched Green at work
on the floor. Who the hell was this barrow boy pleb on the make?
How dare he sell our entire order and then 'low-tick it'. Who the hell
does he think he is? We are Salomon. We are number one. We run
this bloody pit. Does he not know who we are? The rivalry between
the pair only increased over time and went beyond the confines of
the trading floor. When Ersser bought a Ferrari 328, Green went and
bought the more expensive Ferrari Testarossa. I am sure that this
pissed Badger off no end!

Seeing brash working class boys making big money gave some
dealers 'the green eye'. Envious traders who worked for the big banks
would always enjoy watching us suffer if the market moved against
us. One dealer who worked for Goldman Sachs would always try to
make sure we lost money. A favourite trick of his would be to ask
everybody in the pit what they were offering and buy them all
knowing he had another 2,000 lots to buy. This would pretty much

guarantee that all the locals on the floor lost money. He had the power to make sure the price of contracts in the market would trade higher – and not lower – as the locals that had bought from him were banking on.

The locals themselves could also be their own worst enemies. Liffe had a legion of unexceptional traders with egos that refused to let them believe that a place in the elite ranks of traders was not for them. One good year would make them feel invincible. A whole lifestyle would be funded on that back of a belief that every year would be a winning one in the market. More often than not, this was not the case. Money spent on expensive cars, big houses and lavish holidays would leave a trader with nothing to pay a mounting tax bill when luck on the floor ran out. This would leave a dealer in a frantic struggle to stay solvent – the trappings of success would all be sold to pay the taxman. This could mean swapping a brand new Aston Martin car for a beat up 10-year-old Ford.

A favourite saying in the pits was 'there are players and there are stayers'. Trading was as much a mind game as anything else. One dealer who made – and then lost – £100,000 in the space of a week was psychologically broken by the experience. Having begun a promising career which brought with it rewards such as a Porsche 911, he became fixated with the traumatic experience of losing £100,000 in one day. He ended up leaving the market and moving back in with his parents, getting by on a low income and living hand-to-mouth. The worst thing that could happen to a young trader could be to have a big win in the markets early on which was the result of having a lucky punt and not implementing a professional trading strategy. As surely as a drunk losing at the Black Jack table in a casino, that early win would be followed by heavy losses. The history of the exchange was littered with quickly forgotten locals who set up accounts and lost everything in a couple of weeks.

The trading floor could be an unforgiving place. It was never really an easy place to make money. For the hard-working people who chose to make a living in the pits the consequences of failure could be tragic. A trader in the early nineties took his own life when the pressure of a losing position became too much to bear.

7

The Crash of 1987

A hurricane! Not something you quite expect in England. 'It is true. The whole of southern England has been hit by a storm,' said Diane. 'The television news says people have been killed by falling trees and buildings.' As I heard her describe what would later be known as England's Great Storm over a crackling telephone line it all seemed a bit surreal. I told Diane I loved her and that I would be on a plane back to London the next day. When I put the receiver down I had a feeling of unreality. Here I was in a Singapore hotel room on the other side of the planet while 100 mile per hour winds were apparently wreaking havoc across southern England. Had Diane just made this up to get me back home because she was missing me? This sounded too much of a freakish event.

I had just been enjoying the final day of a business trip to Singapore with my friend and fellow trader Chris Wellman. We had been given a tour around the Singapore International Monetary Exchange (SIMEX), a futures exchange which had just been set up three years earlier. The exchange was keen to attract experienced traders from London to help develop its growing derivatives business. Our days were spent on the trading floor while we enjoyed evenings knocking back some cold bottles of Tiger Beer in the city's many bars and pubs. Despite our modest alcohol consumption, the local traders who joined us thought we were a bunch of beer monsters – two pints was all it took for them to get drunk.

The incentives SIMEX offered us were tempting. These included finding us accommodation for free and not charging exchange fees for the first six months. As the plane took off from Singapore's Changi International Airport I contemplated a new life as an ex-pat in Singapore spending long lazy weekends by the pool. I expected to miss the sunshine of the Orient on my Monday morning commute. But any thoughts of a tranquil life abroad would be quickly erased from my mind on my return. This time I would be walking right into the eye of the storm. History would remember the events that unfolded as Black Monday.

I was expecting a busy week after reading some of the weekend newspapers but Black Monday itself was a relatively uneventful day in the Liffe pits. As the New York Stock Market (NYSE) opened at 2:30 our time we had less than a couple of hours trading while shares tumbled before the floor closed at quarter past four. It was not until I arrived home from work and switched on the television news that I started discovering that America's Dow Jones Industrial Average of 30 leading US stocks had plunged 508 points to close at 1738.74. This 22.6% fall still remained the biggest one-day slump of all time at the time of writing.

When I took the early morning train to work the following day I leafed through newspaper headlines which spoke of 'bedlam on Wall Street' and 'carnage' in world markets. Some articles had even drawn parallels with the stock market crash of 1929. This was going to be a tricky day in the office, I thought. Nevertheless, I was still taken by surprise at the sheer scale of share price falls across markets in South East Asia on Tuesday morning. Dealing in Eurodollars on SIMEX had also been particularly busy. When traders in London, Frankfurt and Paris got to their desks they did not wait for the Liffe pits to open and instead started firing orders into SIMEX and there were some sharp market moves. My initial thoughts were that it would be nice to see some action and I hoped things would not subside when trading started. This optimism would soon vanish.

Like two boxers peppering each other with jabs in the feeling out process at the beginning of a big fight the early market orders came in at a brisk but not frantic pace. But rather than settling down after the first quarter of an hour the orders just kept on coming and coming and coming. On a normal day's trading dealers would just work the bid or offer price. This time most orders were hitting the bid or lifting the offer which made dealing increasingly volatile. As I got to work in the Eurodollar pit I looked up at the flashing numbers on the big screen displaying price movements in the FTSE-100 index. Despite having fallen by 10% on Monday, billions of pounds had been wiped off the value of the share index's leading companies within a couple of hours of the market opening. Prices in London were plummeting as fast as they had done in Tokyo. This had already triggered a flight to quality as dealers sought refuge in US dollars and government bonds when shares prices fell. A knock-on effect of this was falling interest rates which was making dealers buy Eurodollars.

The market was starting to get thin and single orders were moving the prices by three to four ticks – this was unprecedented. A scarcity of paper in the pits had forced locals to start widening their prices and a few even stopped quoting altogether. On a normal day the bid and offer would have 500 lots each side of a one-tick market and it would take a few thousand lots to move the market by three or four ticks. The high and low would typically be about seven ticks apart on the day. But today we had already witnessed a 25–30-tick range. I was on auto pilot manically filling orders and by mid-morning I realised that I had already broken my trading record for orders executed in a single day. This kind of thing just should not be happening in the market. Suddenly I had the realisation that I was trading into the unknown. What I knew for sure was that some people on the floor were going to get badly burnt and all my experience might not be enough to stop me being one of the casualties.

A trader from US brokerage firm Dean Witter piled into the pit. 'Offers' he yelled. This call was greeted by silence. The traders on the floor seemed shell-shocked and stood around motionless. 'Six bid offers,' shouted the Dean Witter man. 'Ten offered,' responded a game local. 'Buy it.' Rather than bidding at seven Dean Witter closed the trades instantly. This just seemed ridiculous, or so we thought. The broker appeared like he was on a mission and shouted 'Ten bid offers?' Another cocky local shouted 'Ten at 15'. The Dean Witter trader bought them and bid over for 47 lots. This was crazy. The market had just moved nine ticks on 53 lots. I sensed that the order was finished and waited for the offers to come back into the market. I was one of 10 locals who jumped on him – 'SOLD!' I was left feeling disappointed that I had only managed to get five off in the melee. Surely they were a gift? I expected to make a quick five ticks when the market adjusted itself and assumed this must have been some sort of vacuum. We all then offered at 15 but there was no bid so we low-ticked it to 10. Now 10 was trading on the screens. This meant that any offer that came in would put us into profit. Easy money, or so I thought. A local trading on behalf of Salomon Brothers asked what the market was – eight bid at 12 we answered. Now I was just waiting for him to offer 10 and earn me a tidy profit. 'How many at 12?' he asked. Astonished, I realised that he was a buyer. This left me struggling to comprehend what was going on as the market had just doubled from the six it had been trading at a few minutes ago. The Salomon broker then proceeded to buy every other offer for the next 10 ticks as panic began to take hold on the floor. I had no choice but to pay 25 for my five lots – which left me covering a loss of $1,250 on a five lot in the space of two minutes. The markets had just gone mad!

As I stumbled on the floor I began fielding a barrage of quotes. It felt like every broker and trader in the world was calling the floor to find out what was happening. I looked over my shoulder at the dealing booths. 'John. What the f**k is going on? What's trading?' 'It's all Salomon buying. There's nothing in here,' I explained while hand signalling a flurry of prices to the booths. All hell had just broken lose in the pits and I had stopped seeing the funny side of trading. This was all about survival now. Don't trade for yourself, I kept telling myself. If I don't trade on my own account I can't lose. The market was now 10 ticks wide 20 bid at 30. A broker bought at 30 and before anyone could quote again another dealer came into the pit and sold at 20, netting an instant 10-tick profit. I told myself to move in before it dawned on me that I did not really know what I should be doing any more. What the hell was happening? Rather than trade blindly I decided to cut my size down 20 lot to a 2 lot. I started to make money again. My gut instinct had once again been proved right.

I focused my mind on frantically filling orders for my regular customers. Brokers I seldom dealt with were screaming down my face and pushing new orders my way. This will bury me, I told myself. My heart was beating so fast I felt on the verge of having palpitations. I knew that just one out trade would be enough to bankrupt me. The first hour and a half of afternoon trading had shot by like an exploding bullet. I took a deep breath and waited for the big guns in Chicago to open their pits. The CME was the global centre for dealing in Eurodollars. More than 100 traders were gathered around me in the pit and nobody was quoting now. There was a hushed silence broken intermittently by traders nervously tapping their feet on the exchange floor. My hands shook as I clung to my trading cards. A tremor ran through me and I imagined what a First World War soldier must have felt like before leaving the trenches for 'no man's land'.

The time was now 1:30 and as Chicago opened, the US's Federal Reserve released a statement promising to supply the market with enough liquidity needed to overcome the crisis. This news fuelled the aggression of American banks and brokerage firms. The traders representing these firms wanted to buy at any price. 'Offers,' yelled a dealer from Transmarket. 'Two at 40,' shouted Trevor, a slightly built local. He had called a price 15 ticks above the last trade. 'Buy them,' retorted the Transmarket dealer before shouting '50 for a 100 … 60 for 100.' Another American broker made his presence known '80 bid … 90 bid …' I was left wondering what the hell was going on. Within 90 seconds the prices had moved 200 ticks higher despite there being no dealing volume. Instead of profiting as the market corrected itself, Trevor was forced to buy back his two lots for a $10,000 loss. This was probably the equivalent of two months' trading profits for a small local like him. The little man had just got swallowed by a beast unleashed from across the Atlantic. Trevor looked ashen as he registered the loss. I was just happy that it was not me.

I would later hear that LaPorta had left the pits in despair. He had taken short positions on US treasury bonds after the Fed's announcement which made the markets shudder like a patient absorbing a heavy dose of electric shock treatment. LaPorta had watched in disbelief as the market moved violently in the opposite direction of his positions. Bill, his clerk, would later find him sitting on the steps of the exchange outside with his head in his hands, his pockets still stuffed with the dealing cards which he thought had ruined him.

'We are missing a lot of your trades,' said Bill.
'I am finished. I guess I have lost $55,000,' mumbled a distraught LaPorta. 'Are they still trading at 93?'
'What! Don't you know that they sold off when Wall Street opened and are now trading at 87?' replied Bill.

Treasury bonds had moved six points in the space of 10 minutes. An almost unthinkable event before the autumn of 1987. In a daze LaPorta stuffed his trading cards into Bill's hands and ran back into the exchange to cover his position. After staring down the face of bankruptcy and a lonely trip to the poor house LaPorta went to work on securing a $220,000 trading profit. This was the most money he had ever made on the floor in one day in his life. LaPorta would be forever remembered on the Liffe floor for blowing out and having his biggest ever win on the same afternoon of 20 October 1987.

Rapid-fire orders rattled through the Liffe pits like machine gun fire. My ear drums rang with a cacophony of buy and sell orders which seemed loud enough to shake the roof of the old Royal Exchange building. I could see different prices being offered across the pits as dealers madly pushed and shoved their way to get their orders filled. Nobody knew for sure what the correct price was. Wild gyrations in prices were particularly prevalent in the US Treasury bond pit. One local heard an offer at 15 on one side of the pit and a bid of 25 on the other. He quickly bought the 15 offer and sprinted across to the other side of the pit to sell the 25 bid – netting tens of thousands of pounds in profit within a few seconds. The volatility also created confusion. Two young brokers filling orders for Goldman Sachs on behalf of Kyte were left uncertain how many times a filled order had been confirmed. To their horror, the pair discovered that a big order had been filled twice. This left them sitting on a three quarters of a million pound loss.

Over-analysis will lead to paralysis, I told myself. This was the time to trade on instinct. Like a boxer in the last rounds of a fight who tucks his chin down and unloads leather to keep his opponent at bay I set about trading on instinct, just hoping to get through the day. I had no idea what the spread should be so I left it alone and focused on filling orders for other members. I would later calculate that I had been executing trades at a rate of more than one order every minute for the eight hours I was on the floor. If ever the law of the jungle was ruling the markets it was now. Ackerman stepped into the Eurodollar pit and started making a spread market 20 ticks wide (normally it would be a one or two-tick market). Ackerman usually traded in the short sterling pit but saw a chance to make a killing. If this was the equivalent of diving into the bear pit and beating your chest it paid off for him. He would walk away from the exchange with an alleged six-figure profit that day. When the closing bell rang at 4:15 I was left hunched on the exchange floor, my shirt soaked through with sweat and the top buttons undone. My tie was half way down my chest. I must have looked a mess.

I sat down in the middle of an empty pit and began totting up my trading positions. I was praying that everything would be all square. A clerk asked for a dealing card which I had completed four hours ago – normally a trade was cleared within 15 minutes. Meanwhile, the runners were busying themselves inputting a mountain of trades which had accumulated during the day – they were drowning in paper! 'Has anybody got a card for this 20 lot?' asked a voice nearby. 'Look through this batch,' advised a clerk. I realised that the back office boys had been working flat out too so I started helping out with clearing the trades. This took four hours of painstaking work and by a miracle no errors had been made. I had been on the go for 14 hours non-stop before I finally checked to see that the time was nine o'clock. I heard news that stock markets in the US were on the rebound and the market authorities appeared to be getting the crisis under control. Some clerks would still be on the dealing room floor when I arrived the following morning cleaning up the paper trail from the day's trading. I had made $3,000 trading and filled several thousand lots, consisting of more than 300 orders. This equated to one hell of a paper chain in order confirmations alone. I had survived my busiest ever day on the floor.

Not everyone had been so fortunate. A few months before Black Monday a bearded slack-jaw American trader became infatuated with a young female market maker in the European Options pit. The young beauty caught his eye as she spent her days on the floor waiting to make a market for any paper that might come along. Each day he would pass by and see her disappointed lips pout as she confessed that another day had gone by without any business. The dealer thought her lack of success on the floor presented a great opportunity to get closer to her. What better way to chat her up than to trade with her? He reasoned that regular trips on to the floor to check up on trading positions would be a good way to break the ice. He sold '100 very far out of the money calls' on the basis of a view which had nothing to do with the market spread that day. His generosity was enough to persuade her to have a drink with him but it turned out that she had a boyfriend and was not interested in spreading herself in any other way. Perhaps it was his lack of success on the date which made him blank the trade from his mind. When the market crashed the forgotten trade came back to haunt him. He would lose $150,000 on the deal. His decision to let the options expire rather than make an embarrassing trip back to the European Options pit had proved costly.

8

Cannon Bridge Boom

After nine great years Liffe had moved from the Royal Exchange to a new home in the City at Cannon Bridge. The Queen had been invited to officially open the new exchange floor on 11 February 1992. I had been handpicked as one of 18 traders out of about 3,000 who would meet our country's head of state. I felt honoured. After all, it is not every day that you get to meet the most famous woman in the world. I could tell that my mates on the floor were very jealous. Even guys like Mark Green – who were rarely that impressed about anything – were envious that I had been one of the carefully selected dealers who would meet the royal party. While it may sound amusing that hardened pit traders were so in awe at the prospect of meeting the Queen there was a good reason for it. Many people working on the floor, like myself, had come from quite humble backgrounds. For the working class people that worked at the exchange, meeting the Queen – or even just being present when she visited the floor – had a sort of symbolic importance. For them it meant that it really was possible to be somebody and achieve a position of status in society.

Earlier on in the day of the Queen's visit, a gentleman from the Royal House gave me a briefing on the appropriate etiquette one should adopt when meeting Her Majesty. To say the chap was very posh would have been an understatement. He had slick black hair, wore a dark blue pinstripe suit and had shoes which were so well polished they looked like a couple of walking mirrors. But he did not dwell on formalities when he told me how I should act in the Queen's presence. Her Majesty should be addressed as Mam – just like jam – and never be touched. He instructed me to only speak when spoken to and bow my head when introduced to the Queen. Okay, I think I've got that, I thought.

The Queen arrived at 4:15 after the final bell of the day's trading. Spontaneous applause erupted as the royal party took to the floor. Everybody had stayed behind after work to catch a glimpse of the Queen. If a leading politician visited the exchange he could run the gauntlet of abuse from the floor's locals. When Ken Clarke visited the floor during his tenure as Chancellor of the Exchequer he was greeted with chants of 'Who ate all the pies?' and 'YOU FAT BASTARD'. But there was a hushed and respectful silence as the Queen unveiled a commemorative plaque and accepted the gift of a sterling silver trading badge. Chris Henry, chairman of Liffe's floor committee, escorted Her Majesty around the floor. I stood in line at the edge of the Eurodollar pit and waited for the royal party to approach. There were about 500 people standing behind me and they all started to clap as Her Majesty drew nearer. The next thing I knew, I was conversing with the Queen. For some reason my memory goes blank when I try to recall what was said in the conversation. All I know is that we spoke for several minutes. I do remember that she asked if I had any traders that worked for me. To which I replied 'About half a dozen'. Then for a split second there was an uncomfortable pause. When she did not move away I just carried on talking. About what I do not know! The Queen had such a nice manner and struck me as a very sweet little old lady. The Duke of Edinburgh followed at her side and he made me feel at ease right away. He asked a lot of questions and came across as very knowledgeable about the markets. When I told my parents that I had met the Queen I think it was the only time in my life when they appeared genuinely impressed by something that I had done.

I was sad to leave the Royal Exchange. It was a place of great memories. But surging volumes in futures and options were about to blow the roof off the historic venue. The new home on Cannon Street did not have the imperial splendour of the Royal Exchange. Instead of Greco-Roman pillars, the new venue's entrance was built using black and white marble and it felt pretty soulless in the beginning. Inside was a dealing room floor which covered about 25,000 square feet making it two and a half times the size of the Royal Exchange. The venue was equipped with 614 booths, 1,000 screens and 440 dealer board consoles. One journalist likened the Cannon Bridge exchange to a 'mini Merc'. This was because it housed state of the art technology 'in a modern and bland environment'. But the sanitised, fluorescent-lit floor did a good job of supporting rapidly growing dealing volumes. In January 1992, 5,309,277 contracts were traded – a 67% rise from the 3,358,603 contracts traded in January 1991.

Trading would never be the same again. Just about everybody knew every dealer that worked on the floor in the early days, even if it was just by their nickname or trading badge. This would never happen at Cannon Bridge. When the exchange reached its peak it supported about 4,000 dealers. The bigger trading floor would also herald a new era that was much more cutthroat. As traders started to enjoy their most successful years, a prominent dealer summed up the Cannon Bridge ethos when he said: 'I don't come to work to make friends, I come to work to make money.' It was nobody's job to help a dealer out if he or she made a mistake. A new recruit who messed up a trade would be fired on the spot. He would be sacked because he was incompetent and it was nobody's job to help him out.

The Liffe floor was making a lot of young men rich. For example, the best order fillers were trading 2,000 lots a day or more on commissions of between 50p and a £1 a lot which could add up to an income of about £500,000 a year. Some of these dealers were not about to put the wads of cash that they earned into a retirement or pension plan. High stakes poker games in which Porsches were won and lost at the cards table became part and parcel of the culture of the floor. As were trips to casinos where five-figure sums were won and lost in a single evening. Your word was your bond on the floor and a handshake was used to agree sports bets between dealers that could involve astronomical sums of money. One dealer was forced to sell his house to settle a bet. The expensive house, beautiful wife and desirable sports car were all part of the lifestyle of a successful pit trader. Once a dealer asked a clerk for some ideas of what he could do at the weekend. The clerk suggested that he take his girlfriend to the Ideal Home Show. 'Ideal home. Ideal home. I've got the ideal home you c**t,' replied the dealer. The dealer instead chose to take a long weekend in Rome where he took his girlfriend to the Sistine Chapel. '800 blokes looking at my bird and 50 people looking at Michelangelo's paintings,' was his recollection of the tour around the chapel.

Traders adopted an attitude to the job which much more closely resembled that of traders in the pits of Chicago and a lot of dealers made sure that they stayed in good enough shape to handle the tough physical requirements of the job. The new Cannon Bridge era was not all about health and fitness though. I never personally witnessed any drug taking. But I have been reliably informed that illegal narcotics – which mainly consisted of the use of cocaine – became far more prevalent on the floor. A drugs bust did take place at the exchange. But it happened on a Monday night, which may explain why the police found little evidence of narcotic use. If it had happened on a Friday night it might have been a different story. Some traders stashed wraps of cocaine inside mobile phones and snorted a few lines in the boozer at lunch time. A popular time for the exchange's cokeheads to take a hit would be before the release of a major US economic figure. Snorting a few lines in the toilet before walking on to the exchange floor must have only added to the adrenaline rush of trading. I guess these dealers thought that the euphoric feeling from the drug would give them the confidence to perform at their best in the pits. In reality, traders that regularly took narcotics became more erratic in their dealing strategies and would usually end up losing money. While a small minority of young dealers could burn the candle at both ends and go out on all night drug-fuelled sessions and still perform like a demon in the pits the next day, these characters were the lucky ones. A self-destructive lifestyle could have disastrous consequences for those earning a living in the pits. Unsurprisingly, the star traders of the floor frowned upon any type of substance abuse.

Technology was introduced at the new exchange to monitor dealing. Video cameras were installed across the floor, recording the action in the pits from a variety of different angles. Dealers that were hit with out trades could watch video footage of the sequence of events leading up to the trade. This made it easy to apportion blame. Disputes could easily be settled without the need for an arbitration hearing. When violent confrontations erupted in the pits, video footage also came in handy and could be used as evidence in disciplinary hearings. A dealer would hardly be able to deny punching somebody when it was recorded on film. Dogsy would fall foul of the new big brother environment when he faced a disciplinary panel over video evidence of him punching a Salomon Brothers gilt pit trader for not splitting a trade with him. The hearing ended amicably with the Salomon trader admitting that he had acted unfairly. The pair apologised to each other and were soon best mates again! It was not long before the video tapes were also being used for traders' amusement. Ackerman once lost his footing near the pit and stumbled down four or five steps before collapsing in a heap at the bottom of the pit. The sight of him being sent sprawling on the dealing room floor looked hilarious. Word of the incident quickly spread around the floor. Then, miraculously, about 30 traders all claimed to have had out trades at the same time. A long queue of dealers waited outside the video room to watch the tape that showed action replays of Ackerman's fall.

The larger scale of the Cannon Bridge exchange changed how people traded. Instead of moving around the floor, dealers started to specialise in a particular pit. My Eurodollar pit used to be a prime place to trade but it was now dying a slow death. In September 1984 a mutual offset system started operating between the CME and SIMEX. This cost Liffe a lot of business. To make matters worse, the CME started opening 10 minutes earlier at 1:20 London time. This was a competitive decision because it was 10 minutes prior to the publication of American economic figures. Before the CME changed its opening hours, the release of such figures would bolster trading in Liffe's Eurodollar contracts. A pit which had hosted about 200 traders in its prime now had fewer than 20 traders. This did not hurt me in the pocket because as the volumes shrunk my market share grew, which meant that the profits I earned never dipped. But the fortunes of the Eurodollar pit contrasted with a Euromark pit which had become packed with hundreds of traders dealing thousands of contracts every day. This was the place to be if you were a hungry trader in your early twenties.

I was now 34 and had spent 10 years building up a customer base. During my twenties, I had relished the physical and mental stresses of the job. But it had become harder to maintain the high standards of performance that I had set for myself as the years went by. There was an expression dealers had: would you kill your granny for a tick? As I looked around at the bunch of young hungry dealers working in the pits it dawned on me that the burning hunger which makes you think nothing about jumping around like a mad man and screaming blue murder to get a trade off just was not there anymore. I had to face the facts. Being a trader was hard physical work and in six years' time I would be 40. Less than 1% of dealers in the pits were above this age. It was time for a new challenge so I retired as a full-time trader. I had made a net trading profit of $1.5 million from 1986 to 1992. I filled £400,000 in floor broker-age and together with scratch trade rebates made £1.5 million in total, which can be broken down into an average annual salary of about £250,000. Not bad money at all back in the eighties and early nineties! I am proud to say that I only had half a dozen losing days during this time.

Now my efforts were focused upon building my own business. Hugh had taken more of a back seat, becoming almost a silent partner in Morgan Sussex. Every year he would relinquish more control of the business as we settled our affairs over a few pints in the Simpson's Tavern. The Cannon Bridge exchange had not been open long before Hugh decided to move back to Bermuda. I flew over to the sun-drenched tax haven to see Hugh and we agreed that Morgan Sussex would become Sussex Futures. He gave me his Liffe shares in return for a stake in the new business. Everything was agreed amicably on the first night. We just shook hands on the deal after sinking a few beers. There was no need for any lawyers or contracts. Apart from one visit to the Bank of Bermuda, the rest of the week was spent knocking back beers in the island's many watering holes. I stayed at his picturesque four-bedroom villa which faced on to a quay where some of the island's fine yachts basked in the sunshine. But being Hugh's drinking buddy meant that there was no time for sun bathing or water sports. Not with all that drinking that had to be done! I came back to England with a T-shirt which had a map of all the pubs on Bermuda printed on it. We just about managed to visit every one.

Now I could get to work on turning the plans I had for Sussex Futures into reality. The money and contacts that I had built up during my days on the floor would be used to sponsor other traders and take them under my wing, just like Hugh had done with me. First a dealer had to be found to replace me in the Eurodollar pit. Luckily, big Nigel Clark, a broker at Tulletts, wanted to try his hand as a local and he jumped at the chance when I offered him the opportunity to replace me. Big Nigel was a gentle giant. He weighed in at 24 stone which meant that he did not struggle to have a presence in the pit. The letters BFG adorned his trading badge. This stood for big friendly giant – or big fat git – take your choice. Years later Nigel and another 20-stone plus broker, who had the moniker of Lardy, visited my office one afternoon. After the pair had signed in with the receptionist, a security guard hurriedly called me to tell me that two of the biggest guys he had ever seen in his life were on their way up to see me. 'Are you going to be okay sir?' he asked. I think he thought I was being visited by debt collectors or a pair of heavies hired by a gangster!

Word soon got out that Sussex Futures was looking for traders and it was not long before a team of 20 had been assembled. My contacts helped get my team floor brokerage. Some dealing firms even told traders that business would be offered if they worked for me. I rented some office space above Cannon Street railway station. It was only about 800 square feet, housing five desks. For the first time in my Liffe career I was spending time behind a desk and not on the dealing room floor. It was not all paperwork though. I still came down to the floor on a regular basis to cover for traders that were off sick or having a long lunch. This could be very demanding work as I would be out of the comfort zone of my Eurodollar pit. I might spend 20 minutes in the Swiss pit, half an hour in the Eurolira and finish the day dealing in the ECU pit. While picking up a deck of orders that you were not familiar with was not easy, I felt that if you could trade one market you could trade them all. The same driving principles of fear and greed applied in every situation. I had to support my traders, particularly when dealing got busy. Half a dozen clerks in yellow jackets were now processing orders and reporting to me.

I spotted an opportunity for Sussex Futures to build a niche market offering brokerage services in the pits which had low amounts of dealing volumes such as Eurodollars, Swiss francs, Eurolira and the BTP. Most banks would only employ half a dozen traders to man the major pits. Hiring dealers to carry out brokerage business on their behalf in the less active pits was not commercially viable. But dealers working for Sussex Futures were able to do business for dozens of customers in these pits. Booth brokers preferred giving business to us and it was not long before my boys were making good money. All my traders were employed on a self-employed basis. The best obtained 80% of the income which they generated on the floor without receiving a guaranteed salary. Other dealers traded only on their own account without doing any brokerage business and I would typically take about a fifth of their trading profits.

As time went on I employed an office manager to do the paperwork and a floating trader to cover the pits for me. I was now spending my time generating new business and managing my traders. Business started to explode after JP Morgan asked me to put an elite team together to fill the US investment bank's orders in the new Bobl pit. I approached two of the best traders on the entire floor, David Helps of Cargill and David Roser of GNI – who had the nickname Macca – to come and work for me. This took some work but the promise of business from JP Morgan swung it and they both agreed to join. This was a real coup – I had landed the star traders that I had been looking for. Now all I needed was a floor manager. Brian Moffat, who had served a similar role at Gerald Metals, a commodities firm, fitted the bill nicely. Moffat was from the East End of London and had an ego much bigger than his 5 ft 6 in frame. Football was his passion and he had played for the England amateur youth team in his teenage years. Moffat had experience of managing dozens of locals and also had a similar floor manager role at JP Morgan. I had also decided to branch out into telephone broking as well. When Ersser had a big fall out with his bosses at Salomon Brothers I asked him if he wanted to come and work for me. To my surprise he agreed. Thirteen years on from when he had landed a job which I thought should rightfully have been mine the tables had been turned and I was his boss. It felt like we had travelled full circle. The arrival of Ersser and Moffat generated more broking business. Sussex Futures was becoming a big player in the market. I rewarded the pair with top-dollar salaries. Uninformed observers might have thought that I was spending the money to pay for their drinking sessions. But highly profitable business was agreed while the pair were enjoying a few pints. Who was I to complain? They were making me rich!

I went on to hire Keith Penny as an order filler in the BTP pit. Penny was one of the best order fillers to ever work on the Cannon Bridge floor. Standing 6 ft 7 in tall, Penny had an abundance of all the talents needed to survive in the jungle of the dealing pits. He had a great aptitude for numbers, a cool head, self-confidence and a sharp wit. When one of the top boys in the BTP pit said that all the other dealers in the pit surely wished that they were half the man that he was, Penny quickly retorted: 'I think you will actually find that you are only three quarters of the man that I am.' Nothing else needed to be said. Penny came to see me one night after the close of trading to tell me that he had received an offer from Midland Bank which included a basic salary of £250,000 a year. The bank had been cutting corners employing second-rate order fillers on salaries of £40,000 or £50,000 a year. This mistake was costing it hundreds of thousands of pounds a year in out trades. Midland Bank had belatedly realised that it was cheaper in the long run to offer high salaries to attract the best dealers on the floor. I thanked Penny for keeping me informed as he considered the offer. In the end he would turn Midland Bank down after consulting with his accountant. He told me that he would not be able to afford the pay cut!

Hidden away in a small alley near the exchange was The Bell pub, which became my firm's favourite boozer. Every lunch time the pub would be crammed full of dealers clad in the blue Sussex Futures jackets. My boys took the place over and would be in there talking football, racing and other important matters of the day. Moffat and Ersser regularly summoned dealers to the pub to host strategy meetings. Everything from disciplinary hearings, trading tactics and brokerage deals would be discussed. I would sometimes get a call from Ersser asking me to come down to the pub to seal a deal with another bank. We would agree on a price for floor brokerage business over a few pints.

Mark Adcock, who traded the FTSE pit, rarely joined in with the pub banter, preferring instead to play the trivial pursuits machine while sipping half a pint of lager. He would use his photographic memory to clean machines out every night until he was eventually banned from just about every pub in the area. Employing a guy with a photographic memory and an obsession for trivial pursuits was one thing. But he was by no means the most eccentric character at the firm. For example, one dealer had a constant desire to get naked. On one occasion after a night's drinking he took all his clothes off in the back of a taxi cab. When it stopped at traffic lights he noticed a broken hoover on the side of the road. He jumped out of the car and started using the broken cleaning device to hoover the road while stark naked. The police soon arrived and asked him what he was doing. 'What does it look like, I'm hoovering,' replied the dealer. The next morning I got a phone call 20 minutes before the market opened. He told me that he would be late into work that day as he was still being held at the police station.

Ersser and Moffat would often spend evenings entertaining clients in London's West End while I was at home enjoying some time with Diane. This suited me fine. Once I had won some business with a firm I knew Ersser and Moffat would know what to do to keep our clients happy, though the evenings could sometimes get a little bit messy. Ersser once took a major broker out to dinner at the Savoy. On the next table was seated a group of Japanese businessmen. Late in the evening a smartly dressed member of the neighbouring Japanese party stood up before clearing a space on the table. He then executed a perfect headstand with the poise of a skilled gymnast. As he returned to his seat the restaurant's manager raced over to give him a ticking off. The contrite businessman apologised and asked his eating companions to buy the restaurant's best bottle of champagne. 'I could do that no problem,' said a City trader from the major broker. 'Okay, you're on,' said Ersser who bet him a bottle of the best bubbly in the house that he could not.

The trader was not about to back down from Ersser's challenge. Liffe floor dealers were an ultra-competitive bunch. He cleared a space in front of him on the table and summoned his strength to repeat the Japanese man's acrobatic feat. A hushed silence took hold among the dining tables surrounding him as the other customers waited to witness another headstand. After a promising start, The trader's arms began to wobble as he lurched forward. He made an attempt to hoist himself up. 'Steady, steady …' urged one of his colleagues. The trader then pushed his legs up in an ungainly pose before the pressure on his hands became too much and he fell crashing down on to the table, smashing all the crockery around him. The major broker and Sussex Futures party were promptly billed for damages and escorted from the premises.

My own hunger for the business seemed to filter down to my growing team of traders. The vast majority became successful dealers earning life-changing amounts of money on the way. It was not long before Sussex Futures became serious competition for some of the established corporate brokers in the market. From 1995 onwards, we maintained a top twenty position for pit-filled trading volumes out of about 160 member firms of the exchange. By 1997, there were about 50 traders and 20 runners working for me along with a full-time accountant. Sussex Futures made more than £1.3 million in gross profits that year, leaving me almost £1 million to put in the bank. I took £400,000 for myself, reinvested some in trading shares on Liffe and the rest of the money was left in retained profits to boost the balance sheet. This year was probably when the Cannon Bridge floor – and Sussex Futures – reached a peak. My locals were regularly executing 50,000 lots a day between them. I had overtures from several trading firms who were interested in buying the business. A Dutch trading group and an Italian bank mentioned sums of £5 million. But I loved my firm too much to sell it. A big mistake in hindsight.

Sussex Futures had consolidated its position as one of the leading independent brokers on the floor by the late nineties, recruiting some of the best people around. I poached some top traders, including John Jones and Gary Pert. But I am sure my rivals knew that it was never anything personal and just business. A rival firm entertained its dealers with hookers and cocaine. A penthouse flat in Mayfair was rented out for the firm's Christmas party. 'High class' prostitutes and bowls of cocaine were made available to make sure the guests were kept entertained. I preferred to keep my team of traders loyal by taking them to major boxing, cricket and football events. We would also attend dinners at Grosvenor House and hear sporting celebrities speak, including Kevin Keegan, Henry Cooper and Will Carling. Sport has always been my passion so I did not mind paying for my boys to attend. When Sussex Futures obtained Public Order Member (POM) status – which enabled us to trade with companies that were not members of the exchange – we held a celebratory dinner at which Sir Trevor Brooking, the West Ham football legend, gave a speech. Brooking was great company over dinner. But he was too much of a gentleman to make a compelling after-dinner speaker. The man would never say a bad word about anyone. To make matters worse, there were problems with the microphone which made it difficult for everybody to hear what the great man was saying. At the tail end of his speech a couple of American traders turned up with a London broker. Being American, the pair did not have a clue about who Brooking was and proceeded to talk loudly as he spoke. I walked over and politely asked them to be quiet but they continued to be noisy. The sight of an England football legend being disrespected in this way was all too much for Ersser who decided to take the law into his own hands. He ran over to the noisy latecomers and grabbed the London broker in a headlock causing quite a scene before he was pulled away by diners seated nearby! That event almost proved to be the highlight of the night. Brooking was not a memorable speaker. But what the hell did I care? Being a success in the financial markets was enabling me to meet the football stars that I had cheered on from the terraces at Upton Park as a kid. To me that really was fantasy league football stuff!

9

The Omen

I was sprinting towards the Bobby Moore stand at Upton Park and yelling at one of my traders to give me the ball. He slid in a great pass leaving me with an open shot at goal. The next thing I know I've slammed the ball into the back of the net! What a moment. But this wasn't a dream. Being a big West Ham fan, I had arranged for a Sussex Futures team to play a match at Upton Park against Cargill. This was as close as I was ever going to get to playing for my team. The game took place before West Ham player Tony Gale's testimonial match. This was a dream come true for me – we even got to get changed before the match in the room adjacent to the West Ham changing rooms. The match kicked off two hours before the testimonial. When we ran out on the pitch the only people in the ground were family and friends. But mid-way through the second half the ground did start to fill up so we also had the honour of playing in front of the West Ham fans, who were happy to laugh and jeer at all of our mistakes.

Kyte, an avid Spurs fan, had given me the idea to arrange the match. He had arranged for a game to take place at White Hart Lane a few years earlier. The match took place before Tottenham played West Ham in Ray Clemence's testimonial and I had gone along to watch. Kyte was a good football player, as were Dickinson and Crawley. Both teams had to put up with a fair amount of verbal abuse from the visiting West Ham supporters. My abiding memory was of Mickey Partridge, a massive West Ham supporter from the short sterling pit, who ran over to the away supporters' section of the ground at the end of the match and tore off a replica Spurs shirt to reveal his own Hammers top. He then threw the shirt to the ground and stamped on it, much to the delight of the visiting West Ham supporters. That would be just about all the Hammers' fans would have to cheer about that night. We were torn apart by Spurs that day. Paul Gascoigne terrorised our defence and looked good enough to win the match on his own. I joined the players in White Hart Lane's executive lounge after the match. Here the Liffe boys were joined by Gascoigne and Gary Lineker, the England striker. An auction took place for a signed football which gave Kyte and Dickinson an opportunity to flex their financial muscles and have a go at outbidding each other. The ball must have been sold for about £2,000 in the end!

Rugby player Will Greenwood's experiences while working on the Liffe floor featured in Will, the biography of the former England international. He described his time in the pits as 'one long adrenalin rush' which was exciting and terrifying in equal measure. 'It may sound strange, but there is a good deal of similarity between an international rugby match and a trading session in the City in the days before it became fully computerised: the pressure in both instances is enormous,' writes Greenwood. 'You have to make quick and critical decisions on the hoof, you have to keep a cool head and you need to be bullish and brave. The only major difference between the two worlds as they were back then was that, after a day in the City, you tended not to end up in a big bath together singing lewd songs and throwing soap at each other.'

Unsurprisingly, the pits were crammed full of talented sportsmen. There were dozens of semi-professional football players and an ex-professional in the case of Trevor Putney, the former Ipswich Town player. Russell Kean, who was probably one of the best non-league players around, allegedly had both Southend and Spurs offer him professional terms. Kean turned the clubs down because he could not afford to take a pay cut. How times have changed! Even City traders are jealous of the wages that some of the top Premiership football players now earn. The floor also played host to international cyclists, basketball players and scratch golfers. Dealers had to have a certain amount of physical conditioning just to be able to keep up with the demands of the market. This involved fending people off from their trading spot and dealing flat out on their feet for eight hours every day. I believe we could have got a football team together that would have given a League Two professional team a very good game.

The tough demands of trading meant that if you were a keen martial artist, it would not do you any harm in the pits. There were a few amateur boxers working on the floor along with a judo champion. A sandy-haired trader named David Flowerday took up boxing and soon became quite handy in the noble art. He trained at the St Pancras Amateur Boxing Club in Kings Cross. Once a year the boxing club hosted a charity boxing evening at the Brewery, a conference centre located on Chiswell Street in the City. The event was always packed to the rafters with Liffe dealers who took over all the tables near ringside. Flowerday was on the evening's card fighting as a lightweight. When he made his way to the ring the venue reverberated with chants of 'Oh Davy Flowerday, Davy, Davy, Davy, Davy Flowerday.' I felt sorry for the other kid. He was never going to get the decision. It was no surprise when the judges gave Flowerday the nod after the fight went the distance. An auction of sporting memorabilia followed hosted by the television presenter Jeremy Beadle. When I first saw Beadle appear, I had feared for the TV funny man. He had one deformed little hand which was enough to make him the object of ridicule among some of the gathered Liffe dealers. Serious drinking had gone on by this time. But Beadle was unfazed by the mob of drunken traders and did a great job of making the big trading houses and locals bid against each other. 'The mighty Salomon Brothers is surely not going to be outbid by this humble little money broker?' jested Beadle on his way to raising thousands of pounds for charity.

An even bigger Liffe following made the trip to the Café Royal in London's West End for Flowerday's next contest. Incessant chanting of the name Davy Flowerday echoed around the famous Regent Street establishment all evening. The promoters of the show were wise to the fact that a few hundred Liffe traders were drinking the place dry as they waited for Flowerday to fight so they put the Liffe man top of the bill. His opponent was a tough-looking bloke from the north of England who sported a few tattoos. No sooner had the referee announced the start of round one, Flowerday was knocked spark out for the count of ten. The northerner then jumped on to the ropes and called the army of Flowerday fans out for a fight as well, waving uncomplimentary hand gestures at them. The north–south divide lives on! When Flowerday returned to work on Monday floor traders greeted him with the words 'seconds out, round one … one, two, three, four, five, six, seven, eight, nine, ten …' The catchphrase 'done a Flowerday' was used whenever a dealer fell over in the pits from that day onwards.

A group of hapless anti-capitalist demonstrators found out just how tough some of the people on the floor were when they attempted to storm the Cannon Street building and get on to the trading floor in 1999. We had already been informed by the police that day about the risk of protestors targeting us in our coloured jackets. We were advised not to wear our trading jackets in the streets. But we were all proud of the job that we did so nobody bothered to take this advice. An angry mob gathered outside the entrance of the exchange in the afternoon. Windows were smashed and the front of the exchange building was daubed with some paint by the protestors. Some managed to barge their way past the police and security staff and made their way up the escalators to the dealing room floor. Blocking their path was Gripper, a former member of West Ham's infamous hooligan Inter City Firm (ICF), and a dealer who had served in the Foreign Legion. The demonstrators had come to the right place if they wanted a fight! Several would need hospital treatment and needless to say nobody made it through to the exchange floor. The pair of trading floor 'bouncers' were summoned to the chairman's office on the following Monday morning. Both Gripper and the ex-

Legionnaire feared an instant dismissal for their actions, or perhaps even being taken away by the police to face charges of grievous bodily harm. Instead the chairman took it on himself to personally thank the pair for their heroic actions of defending the exchange against the violent protestors!

One of the perks of being a success in the futures business is being able to step into worlds that you would never come close to if you were doing a normal nine-to-five job. I have always been fascinated by boxing. While I have never climbed though the ropes myself – one look at my nose will tell you that much – I have always been a big fan. I religiously read Boxing News, the sport's trade magazine, and regularly attend big fights. My father was also a boxing fan and the sport has always been an important part of the culture of London's East End. Bethnal Green's York Hall is steeped in boxing history and has staged contests down through the ages involving local boys that have gone on to become world champions. A teenage Mike Tyson would spend hours watching black and white footage of East End fighters like Jack 'Kid' Berg, who was known as the 'Whitechapel Windmill' and used supreme boxing techniques to win the world junior welterweight title in the thirties.

An appeal of boxing to me is that the sport can never be called a game. People do not play boxing. When you turn up to a boxing show you will often see an ambulance waiting on stand by outside, ready to attend to a stricken fighter should the worst happen. Every boxer who steps through the ropes knows that he is putting his life on the line for the entertainment of the crowd. Neurologists will tell you that the inside of a human skull has sharp edges which rip blood vessels apart and bash the soft tissues of the brain when it is rocked about inside the skull after a punch to the head. The slurred incoherent speech of some ex-fighters is a testament to the damage which taking too many blows to the head can do. Sadly my love for the sport would bring the reality of the risks which fighters face all too close to home.

I was introduced to Jess Harding, who had fought for the British heavyweight title, by Ersser. You did not have to be a genius to see that Harding had been a heavyweight boxer. He stood 6 ft 5 in tall and probably weighed about 17 stone. He had a short skinhead hair cut and came across as a quietly spoken nice guy, despite the fact that he could pass for a gangland heavy in a dodgy gangster movie. Harding was working as a manager and boxing promoter. He told me that he was looking for some sponsorship for a young fighter he had recently signed. The lad was a super bantamweight from North London named Spencer Oliver. The dark haired Oliver fought under the name 'The Omen'. Harding had chosen this name because he thought that Oliver looked just like the young innocent Damien in the film *The Omen* – before metamorphosing into a demonic warrior when he did battle in the ring. Coincidently, Harvey Stephens – who played Damien in the horror film – would work for me a few years later.

Oliver had won a silver medal at the 1994 Commonwealth Games a year earlier and Harding was adamant that the lad had what it took to become a world champion. I was not so sure about becoming involved though, which made me hesitate about signing up to a sponsorship deal. In the end I agreed. Harding only wanted £200 a month to cover Oliver's training expenses before his purses got bigger. Oliver had just three fights under his belt at the time and would always be way down on the undercard when I first started taking my son to watch his fights. Attending boxing matches at venues like the Goresbrook Leisure Centre in Dagenham and the Furzefield Leisure Centre in Potters Bar is a long way from the glamour of the sunset strip of Las Vegas. But Harding would always make sure that my boy and I had ringside seats and passes to the VIP lounge. I was starting to enjoy being a part of the boxing business. The sport is not short of personalities. I got to meet Barry Hearn, the boxing promoter, and some well-known fighters. My son would be the only child in the VIP area and he had fun getting autographs from celebrities of the sport and chatting to characters like Ronnie Davis, who trained the enigmatic middleweight boxer Chris Eubank. Watching Oliver fight also gave me a good return on my £200-a-month investment. His all-action style reminded me of a young Barry McGuigan and he was making a chopping block of everyone he fought. Out of the first six fights I watched, five ended inside the distance with Oliver stopping his opponent. It only took nine professional contests before he was up against Patrick Mullings for the Southern Area super bantamweight title.

Mullings was already being touted as a future contender on the world stage and the fight was scheduled to be screened live on Sky Sports. By now Oliver was fighting with the Sussex Futures logo emblazoned on his shorts. The fight itself turned into a war in which both boxers absorbed their fair share of punishment. It went right to the final round before Oliver took control and stopped his opponent. The contest would win the Best Contest of the Year trophy at the British boxing awards. Mullings would later go on to win the IBO super bantamweight world title and the Commonwealth featherweight crown.

It was at this time that Jack Wigglesworth, the chairman at Liffe, told me that the Chicago Board of Trade wanted the exchange to send over a boxer to compete in its annual boxing event. He asked if I would be able to find someone to represent the exchange, given that I was knowledgeable about the sport. This was at a time when relations between Liffe and the CBOT were at a low point. I felt that our friends in Chicago had changed the goal posts on a deal earlier in the year and now I discovered that the CBOT had an American Golden Gloves champion working on the floor who was ready to give one of our London boys a whooping. I am sure that our American cousins would have thought that it was not very British to send a world-class professional boxer to fight against one of their floor workers but I could not resist. Oliver flew over to Chicago representing Liffe and gave the Golden Gloves champion a boxing lesson. He later told me that the American was a good open-class amateur and he had just played with him a bit. Oliver was a gentleman in and outside the ring and he was not going to knock the living day lights out of an enthusiastic amateur who had been matched against someone out of his league.

Oliver returned from Chicago to find out that he was close to a crack at the European super bantamweight title held by the Bulgarian Martin Krastev. Harding said the champion was prepared to defend his belt in London. All he had to do was get the money together to make the fight happen. Harding asked if I would co-sponsor the fight with the Daily Star. When I mentioned the proposal to Ersser, he thought it would be a great way of entertaining our clients and giving the traders a treat so I agreed. I paid £5,000 for 50 ringside tickets. While Oliver had got his shot at the title, not everyone was convinced that he was ready to step up to this level. Colin Hart, a well-known boxing journalist for *The Sun*, made a point of questioning whether Oliver had been brought along too soon at the pre-fight press conference. The bookmakers had the champion down as a clear favourite. I was incredibly excited about the fight. Oliver had almost become a friend by now. Seeing him become a success had become very important to me.

When the night of the fight arrived I felt almost sick with nerves. The feeling I get before West Ham play in a big match just could not compare – and I have been a fanatical Hammers fan all my life. I felt a shiver go down my spine as the MC began the introductions. 'Ladies and gentlemen, welcome to the main event of the evening ... For the super bantamweight championship of Europe ... Sponsored by the *Daily Star* and Sussex Futures.' Oliver had attracted a big following by now. The actor Sean Bean was a couple of seats away at ringside and many of the raucous fans at the back clearly identified with Oliver as being one of their own. He did not disappoint. From the opening bell Oliver went on a seek-and-destroy mission putting the champion down twice in the second round before stopping him in the fourth. Fantastic! Harding made a special point of thanking Sussex Futures in the post-fight television interview which I thought was a nice touch. He said the north had Naseem Hamed and the south had Spencer Oliver. A world championship fight now beckoned. He had graduated from a four-round fighter to European champion in just over two years.

Oliver could now command a sell-out crowd at Kensington's Royal Albert Hall and Alexander Palace, which majestically looms above the North London sprawl. But I had no intention of being squeezed out of the 'Omen' road show now Oliver had become a ranked world title contender. He was close to challenging the tough Mexican Erik Morales for the WBC super bantamweight title. A domestic north vs south scrap with Manchester's Michael Brodie – which would unify the British, Commonwealth and European titles – was also being mooted. Brodie's millionaire manager Jack Trinkett asked Harding if he was interested in a £20,000 bet on the fight, given that he was so confident that Oliver would win. When Harding asked me what I thought about this I did not have time to reply before Ersser interrupted and said: 'Tell him to make it £40,000 and he has a bet. Don't worry John and I will cover it.' I could only smile. Thanks Ted, I thought.

Before Oliver had a chance to fight Brodie or challenge for a world title he had to make a routine defence of his European belt against Ukrainian Serguei Devakov. The bout took place at the Royal Albert Hall and I had agreed to sponsor the event. The VIP lounge was very plush and early on in the evening Harding asked if a couple of his guests could hang out there. Sure I said and was promptly introduced to the pop singer Robbie Williams and Nicole Appleton from the girl band All Saints. I had bought tickets for 50 of the best ringside seats for my guests. After mingling in the VIP area I returned with a friend to ringside to find Jamaican heavyweight and former British champion Gary Mason lounging in our seats. Mason might well have been good enough to challenge for the world title if he had not had the misfortune of being around at the same time as Lennox Lewis, who would later reign as undisputed heavyweight world champion. Lewis had taken seven rounds to stop the big man and I had heard that he was not always the most friendly person you could hope to meet. A pushy fan had niggled him at the wrong moment and allegedly once asked him who he would be fighting next. Mason replied: 'You if you don't get out of my way.' This story made me a little nervous about asking him to move out of our seats. My friend showed Mason his ticket and diplomatically explained that it was his seat. Mason's response was to stare him down, for what seemed like ages. Forget it, I thought. Let the big man sit there. Then Mason got up and said 'of course, no problem' before walking away.

Oliver's loyal following had once again packed out the venue and cheered loudly when he made his walk to the ring as a 50-strong

choir sang the theme tune to *The Omen*. Lasers beamed and fire-
works exploded. Fantastic! All Oliver had to do now was to win, just
like he had done in his 14 previous professional fights. He stepped
out for the opening bell and started measuring up his foe. I felt confident that I was about to witness another victory. Nothing seemed
out of the ordinary as the fighters started to engage. Suddenly a flash
knockdown sent Oliver crashing to the canvas. What the hell was
going on? Oliver gamely got back on to his feet but he never looked
the same afterwards. His timing and strength was just not there. He
looked like he was fighting in a dream. Oliver lasted until the eleventh
round before collapsing after being cuffed around the head with a
light punch. While he managed to drag himself back up at the count
of nine the referee stopped the fight. My disappointment at the
outcome of the contest was soon replaced by feelings of dread when
Oliver slumped prostrate on to the canvas. Something was seriously
wrong. Oliver was not fighting for any title now – he was in a fight
for his life. I knew this in my guts. Years earlier I had met the surgeon
that attended to Michael Watson, a boxer who came close to death
in a super middleweight world title fight against Eubank. I had been
among a group of traders who gave a day's profit to help launch the
British brain and spine foundation. The surgeon told me how crucial
sedation and time was when a fighter suffers a blood clot to the brain.
The paramedics and ring doctors did not waste any time. After 15
minutes of treatment he was taken to Charing Cross Hospital, unconscious and wearing a neck brace. He would soon be undergoing
surgery in a neurological ward.

I was left racked with a terrible guilt. I had encouraged this young
lad to do this. Now he was close to death, or a life blighted by blind-
ness or having to live in a wheelchair. As I nervously spoke to people
in the VIP lounge afterwards my thoughts were lost with the boxer
I had promoted. What a price for a night's entertainment. How could
I have let myself play any part in this sport? I had hired a mini bus
to take friends and family back to Basildon and I never said a single
word during the long journey back home.

When I woke up the next morning Oliver's plight had made television news and the front page of many of the Sunday newspapers. His

injuries were described as 'potentially life threatening'. I was feeling terrible. I just could not stop asking myself how I could have encouraged him to fight. Oliver underwent three hours of surgery during which time a blood clot was removed from his brain. The neurosurgeon who performed the operation said the blood clot was caused by a torn blood vessel at the back of his brain. Oliver was then kept unconscious for two days while doctors waited for his condition to stabilise. Nobody knew what state he would be in when he was brought round. I could not sleep properly while knowing his life and health was hanging in such a perilous state.

Thankfully, Oliver came out of the induced coma in perfect health. I went to visit him in the hospital later in the week where I found him conversing and walking around like nothing had happened. But his shaven head which sported a train-track scar of stitching told its own story. Oliver said that he could not remember anything after the first-round knock down. But rather than just being grateful to be alive he was gutted that he would never be able to box again. He said he would do it all again tomorrow. A few years later he confided that he would lace up his gloves straight away if he was given a licence to box again. Never mind the mortal danger to his health. Boxers are a breed apart! Oliver has since rebuilt his life. He works as a personal trainer for white collar boxers in the City and is a boxing pundit on the Sky Sports television channel. While I remain a boxing fan I would never take part in the business side of the sport again. I had let myself get too involved. Putting myself through the sort of anguish that I had felt when Oliver had been stricken in a coma was a risk I was not prepared to take again.

10

Crimes and Misdemeanours

The odd Hollywood film may portray the dealing room floor as being like a den of thieves, with everybody trying to 'rip each others' faces off'. But the reality was that the Liffe floor did a very good job of policing itself. Cheating and unethical behaviour was frowned upon by the vast majority of dealers. I always played fair and was never involved in any breaches of exchange rules during my 17-year career at Liffe. Apart from a couple of small fines for minor infringements of dealing procedures the traders who worked for me also stayed on the right side of the law. The two exceptions to this resulted in my firm becoming embroiled in major disciplinary actions. On both occasions, dealers that worked for me had been involved in major breaches of exchange rules. But there would be a marked contrast in my sympathies for those involved in each incident.

The first time a dealer of mine landed in hot water with the exchange's disciplinary panel was in the early nineties. JP Morgan had asked if one of my brokers could deal on its behalf in the highly volatile BTP pit. The US investment bank had a team of about 15 traders to cover the floor but being the biggest dealer in the market meant that it would often find itself in desperate need of locals to fill its paper when it was understaffed. If any firm was going to give out brokerage business to Sussex Futures it would be in the treacherous Italian government bond pit. This meant that the pit fillers I employed had to be among the very best in the business.

My firm was under a lot of pressure when JP Morgan asked for help. But I could not say no. I did not want to miss out on the opportunity of more lucrative JP Morgan business. This was good money, typically generating profits of between £3,000 and £4,000 a day. The only problem was that I did not have a senior BTP trader free and I just could not afford the risk of putting a junior trader in a pit where dealing could be so fierce. I asked Darren Summerfield, my best trader in the Swiss Franc pit, if he would do me a favour and fill JP Morgan's orders for me. Summerfield had the nickname 'hissing Sid', because he had a very faint lisp. I told him that it would be a nice little earner for him as he would obtain 80% of the commission. This could add up to £10,000. Not bad money for three days' work! Summerfield did say that he was worried about getting stung with costly out trades. But he agreed to help.

When Summerfield got to work in the BTP pit he was soon swimming hard. Turbulent market conditions were making even the most experienced traders in the pit struggle. JP Morgan was throwing a flurry of orders at him. Even after I sent a junior trader over to back him up he still suffered a few costly out trades. While he was making a fortune in commission he was losing it all in out trades. The floor manager at JP Morgan recognised that these were very tough trading conditions and he took Darren aside and told him that he appreciated his efforts and promised to compensate his errors. This would usually mean that a bank would allow the broker to keep some of the improved fills. This is when the trouble started. For some inexplicable reason, Summerfield decided not to give up a 100 lot contract he had bought for JP Morgan and when the market went up he sold the lots for an £8,000 profit. This was a clear breach of market regulations because the contracts had been bought for a customer yet he had withheld them for his own account. Summerfield thought that JP Morgan would not mind the transgression after the conversation that he had had with its floor manager. After all, Summerfield reasoned, he had lost a similar sum in out trades. This was stupid logic and unfortunately for him a rival broker had seen what he had done and reported the incident to the pit officials. An investigation of the paper chain and video camera footage provided evidence to back up the broker's accusation. Summerfield was now in serious trouble.

Summerfield was hauled in front of the exchange's disciplinary panel, which was chaired by a member of the Liffe board of directors who heard the case alongside two officials from the floor committee. The hearing was conducted in a court room environment with the Market Investigation Department (MID) acting as the prosecution. A legal secretary worked on behalf of the panel. Summerfield had put in a not-guilty plea and hired Eric Bettelheim, a high-powered barrister to defend him. Liffe traders would often hire the best lawyers to defend them in cases at the exchange. On one occasion, Cherie Blair represented two traders accused of breaching the rules of the exchange. She lost and both traders were handed down fines and a suspension. She would never be involved with a case at Liffe again.

The evidence against Summerfield looked compelling. This left me with the choice of assisting the MID in its investigation – which meant not concealing a breach of market rules – or defending Summerfield despite his transgression. I decided to let the case take its own course. I let Summerfield conduct his own defence and told my staff that if anyone had to provide evidence in the case the only obligation would be to tell the truth as a legal witness. Bettelheim, who had recently beaten an MID charge for another client, put up a pugnacious defence of his client. But no amount of legal manoeuvring was going to be enough to get Summerfield off the hook. Witness statement after witness statement proved that he was guilty. The final death nail in Summerfield's City career was delivered by Ersser, my floor manager, who revealed some damning evidence under cross-examination. The case was lost but Bettelheim doggedly stuck to defending his client which further alienated the panel, who appeared to feel patronised by him.

It was no surprise when the guilty verdict was delivered. What did shock me was the three-year ban and £10,000 fine handed down to

Summerfield. To add insult to injury, the panel then fined Sussex Futures £10,000 on the grounds that I had failed to assist the panel in its prosecution and was therefore also guilty. Summerfield was a bit bewildered after the case and could not understand why I had not told him what Ersser was going to say in the hearing. I told him that I had no idea what Ersser would do. Two years of work and tens of thousands of pounds in legal fees had just been poured down the drain. Summerfield's career in the City was over and I felt awful for him. All I could do was pay him the most I could as severance, without raising suspicions that it was a pay-off and I had something to hide. Summerfield would live to fight another day though and he has since carved out a successful career in publishing.

The next time I appeared before the exchange's disciplinary panel I would be feeling nothing else but anger and a burning desire for justice to be done. After all, one of my dealers had got blind drunk and decided to take great punts on the financial markets which could have left me bankrupt. That's the thing about derivatives. They can just as easily be used as super-charged gambling machines as sophisticated financial instruments to manage – and reduce – financial risks. On a Tuesday afternoon in October 1996, an employee of mine decided to behave in just the same way as a loser at the casinos in Las Vegas – get blind drunk and try and make a fortune.

The employee, who will remain nameless, had already carved out a successful career in the BTP pit and was recommended by a respected senior dealer at my firm. I recruited him in the same year that the incident took place. He deposited £50,000 and was allowed to trade from the Sussex Futures office. He agreed to obey a trading limit of 50 lots. The trader made a nice steady start. He would phone his orders down to our booth on the exchange floor and it was not long before he started generating some good business. He was obviously very knowledgeable and a capable dealer who was handling himself well in the market. I certainly had no inkling that he posed a mortal threat to my business.

One day in October he took a boozy lunch at Swithins, a wine bar near the exchange. This in itself might sound like outlandish behaviour for a professional dealer in the financial markets but I can assure you that it was not that unusual in the City of London during the nineties. This meant nobody was that concerned when he did not come back to the office that afternoon. Meanwhile, the dealer was getting paralytic on booze and probably felt – like many a drunk on a Friday and Saturday night – that he could take on the world. He remembered that he had a small position to cover in the markets at about 5:30 in the afternoon. Instead of calling a broker at my firm, he telephoned a broker at GNI to place an order on the after-hours Automated Pit Trading (APT) system. When he was told that the market had rallied, instead of buying back his small position he sold more contracts. He called the broker back again expecting the market to have fallen so he could take his profit and go home but the market had not moved so he decided that he would help it on its way by spoofing some big sell orders. The Liffe panel would later conclude: 'That his [the dealer's] recollections of the incident had been confused by his consumption of alcohol and found that the floor manager of Sussex Futures had instructed him to reduce his positions in the BTP futures contract.'

The drunk ignored the instructions of my floor manager and started offering 1,000 lots on the offer, which he believed would push the market to trade lower and allow him to take his profit. But instead he ended up selling more on his offer and the more he sold, the more aggressively he 'spoofed' his offer in an attempt to artificially move the price of the BTP down with the aim of making purchases to cover his outstanding short positions. The rogue dealer moved up to 5,000 lots and then 9,999 lots, the maximum volume allowed. The fact that 50 lots would have been a big position for a local trader in the BTP pit at that time demonstrates just how far out in the stratosphere his alcohol-addled mind had got him. The disciplinary panel would later conclude that from this time onwards the dealer 'had not appreciated the consequences of his actions'. Eventually, just before the trading session closed senior management from GNI refused to take any more orders from him but by this time he had built up a short position of 699 lots. This was a huge position 14 times above his trading limit. If he had been filled on his 10,000 lot order I could have lost millions of pounds and ended up bankrupt.

By the time I was told about the short position which the dealer had accumulated it was impossible for me to trade out of the position until the next morning. It was really tough to switch off and forget about the massive risk I was exposed to overnight. I had little choice but to try to sleep peacefully as the contracts remained open. Luckily the market opened a little lower in the morning and I quickly scratched a profit of £60,000. Now my thoughts turned to retribution. The dealer had to be punished. He was fired on the spot for breaching the trading limits that we agreed and I deregistered him from the exchange and the Securities and Futures Authority (SFA).

Liffe would now take action against the rogue trader for bringing the market into disrepute. This time I was right behind the MID. In the end my firm had actually made money from the incident, but this made no difference to me at all. No one was going to start gambling with my livelihood and get away with it. The dealer hired a top barrister to defend himself and pleaded not guilty to breaching trading limits and bringing the market into disrepute. His barrister did a spirited job of arguing his client's case as we heard the arguments and witness statements on the day of the trial. Then the telephone tapes were played and the panel heard the drunken slurred words of a man so intoxicated he was clearly not in control of his faculties. All his highly paid barrister could do was repeatedly bang his head on the table while the tape played. The barrister then asked for an adjournment – the game was up. My former trader was hit with a fine of £10,000 and was suspended from the exchange for three months. Sussex Futures was given an 'absolute discharge' by the exchange's disciplinary panel.

11

Bubble

My two brushes with the disciplinary authorities at Liffe in cases involving employees of mine taught me a lot. But as far as the public was concerned, these types of incidents were just part and parcel of the world of finance and nobody really understood or cared what went on. People across the world would only wake up to risks posed by derivatives when a lad from Watford single-handedly bankrupted one of the world's most famous banks. The words 'rogue trader' are synonymous with one man – Nick Leeson. He is not the first or last man to lose hundreds of millions of dollars on the financial markets. Others have followed similarly destructive paths. The most recent example at the time of writing was that of Jerome Kerviel, a judo enthusiast who somehow managed to accumulate losses of €4.9 billion right under the noses of the senior management of Société Générale in the investment bank's Paris head office. But it is Leeson in his bright yellow and black jacket – worn famously by the actor Ewan McGregor in the film *Rogue Trader* – who comes to the mind of most British people when criminal dealing on the capital markets is mentioned.

The Liffe market had opened more than a decade before Leeson's reckless gambling blew up Barings. But derivatives remained a mystery to much of the City of London's top brass even in 1995. Peter Baring, chairman of Barings, once famously opined that 'it was not actually terribly difficult to make money in the securities business.' As an experienced financial futures trader I find it incredible that Leeson was able to get away with his scams for so long. His dealing strategy simply involved putting losing trades into arbitrage positions and writing options to take the premium as a way of covering his losses. I feel confident that I would have sensed there was something wrong quite quickly if I had seen the financial statements from the bank's Singapore operations.

The fact that many people in the world of finance did not have a clue how futures and options worked heightened the sense of bewilderment in the aftermath of the £827 million losses at Barings. How could this happen? How could a wide boy from Watford bankrupt the Queen of England's bank? A knock-on effect of this sense of disbelief has been that more has been written about Leeson's catastrophic dealing than any other rogue trading incident. There has been speculation about whether Leeson siphoned off millions for himself or had an accomplice. People have even questioned whether the senior management at Barings really were in the dark about Leeson's infamous Error Account 88888 as the losses ratcheted up. I am certain that Leeson did act alone without making a single penny from the collapse of Barings. But I also believe that an important piece of the jigsaw in the Leeson story has been overlooked in what has been written about the man so far.

To truly understand the Nick Leeson story you need to know the Mark Green story. Leeson desperately wanted the image of a ballsy star trader. To him this meant one thing – becoming a Mark Green. Green personified the supremely confident dealer that had the swagger of a man both feared and respected by his peers. When Leeson started his career as a trader Green was the most successful local in Liffe's biggest pit, the Euromarks. His ability on the floor gave him the swagger of a man who could corner the market and take on anyone to make a trade go his way. This is exactly how Leeson appeared on the SIMEX floor. Nobody had a clue that beneath the image of a star trader was the reality of a man drowning in an ocean of terribly misjudged trades.

In Leeson's autobiography, *Rogue Trader*, it is clear that he is very impressed with Green's persona. A chapter in the book describes a boozy session the pair had with their wives in the Irish city of Cork during the Christmas holidays. After drinking 10 pints of Murphy's stout during an all-day session Green decided it was time to move on to the next pub. 'I want to stay here,' protested Leeson. But Green was having none of it.

'How much would they [any new customers] spend,' Green asked the pub's owner.

'I don't know. They'd just have a few jars,' he replied.

'They wouldn't spend more than £50 would they?' enquired Green.

'Er, no,' the barman said.

'Well here's £100,' said Green. 'Don't serve any more drinks tonight, particularly to that gentleman over there,' he ordered while pointing a finger at Leeson. 'Now, let's move on,' said Green. 'You've really got to keep up.' Green was a man used to doing things his way. The pair would go on to visit half the pubs in the city. The evening ended with Leeson dashing to his room at the bed and breakfast to escape Green who chased after him with a fire extinguisher.

When Green was on form there was no stopping him. He was an avid West Ham supporter as well and we ended up getting season tickets together. Green would park his Ferrari near Upton Park stadium and pay some local youths £20 to mind the vehicle for the day. We would then usually go for a drink before the game. The pubs around West Ham's ground are not among the most genteel in London. But Green would walk up to the bar like he owned the place. I guess you could say he had the swagger of a working class hero. On one occasion the pub we chose to drink in was ram-packed with thirsty Hammers fans just before kick off. I took one look and said I just could not be bothered to queue for a pint. But Green was unperturbed. He just shouted to a chap standing at the front of the bar – who happened to be a heavily built skinhead with tattoos

– 'Oi mate, get yourself a drink and while you're at it get me two pints of lager as well!' I was waiting for the chap – or another punter standing in front of us in the queue – to tell Green in no uncertain terms to 'f**k right off' as he waved a £20 note in the air. This was not a City of London wine bar. This was the East End of London. There are unspoken rules which have to be obeyed. The wrong look or an accidental shove can sometimes leave you on the brink of a violent confrontation. But Green's magic touch was not about to let him down here. Our new skin-headed friend took the note, made the order and chased after Green with the drinks and change. Unbelievable!

Leeson rejoiced in being seen as just the sort of stellar dealer that Green was. He loved the respect that he got from a man like Green. I do not think he could stomach the thought of Green knowing that he was a fraud and not a superstar trader like him. I think Leeson was a competent guy who just wanted to do his best. He probably could have made a living as a local on the Liffe floor. But he tragically discovered – like so many other dealers whose names will never be remembered – that the talents of the best traders are as rare as those of first-class professional athletes. Without exceptional natural ability it was impossible to reach the highest levels of excellence on the dealing room floor. He got in way over his head and could not face the prospect of letting so many people close to him down.

Leeson got to know Green through a dealer named Danny Argyropoulos. Danny's Greek Cypriot heritage earned him the nickname Bubble (Bubble and Squeak: Greek) and his surname on his trading badge was re-named Viz, after the adult comic. No one was going to remember how to pronounce Argyropoulos. I first got to know Danny when he started working on the exchange. I supervised him in the Eurodollar pit when he was a trainee blue button. When the collapse of Barings thrust fame upon him a newspaper article described him as a pony-tailed broker who was 'teetotal' and 'immensely energetic'. Green was Danny's mentor and he aspired to the brash, lavish lifestyle of the Euromark pit's top boy. When Danny qualified as a trader, Green said that instead of a Christmas bonus he could have the privilege of borrowing his Ferrari. Green would put him on his insurance. This choice was a no-brainer for Danny. He just could not resist the chance of being able to show off in such a flash car. He regularly took Green up on the offer until one fateful day in the summer of 1992. It was the eve of the General Election. The British public were about to once again reject a Labour party led by Neil Kinnock in favour of the grey man of politics, John Major, who would succeed in persuading people to re-elect his Conservative Party. But Danny was not spending the evening agonising over which way to cast his vote at the ballot box. He was showing off on the streets of London taking Green's car for a spin. As he made his way around the capital's West End he noticed that two big guys were following him in a Vauxhall Vector. This made Danny panic. Hadn't there recently been a recent spate of car jacking incidents in London? What if these guys were a couple of gangsters preparing to do him in? Danny's survival instinct kicked in and he put his foot down on the accelerator in an attempt to lose the Vauxhall stalking him. But to his dismay, the car remained hot on his tail. This called for evasive action. He made a sharp turn down a side street. But as Danny swerved around the corner he lost control of the vehicle and hit the curve before smashing into a bus stop sign. Now he didn't give a monkey's if he was being chased by car jackers or not. At least they would put him out of his misery. When Green discovered the wreck that he had made of his beloved Ferrari he would be a dead man.

As Danny leapt out of the car to survey the damage he saw the Vauxhall pull up behind him. When the door of the car opened, the would-be car jackers turned out to be police officers in an unmarked car. Once the pair had confirmed that he was authorised to drive the vehicle they apologised for spooking him and went off on their way. Danny was left to look over the dented Ferrari and contemplate how he was going to break the news to its owner. His response to the situation was measured and reasonable. The following evening he was on a plane leaving the country. Fleeing London for his native Cyprus would give Green some time to cool down.

Danny had only been back in Cyprus a couple of days when staff at the hotel he was staying at told him there was a telephone call for him. Green had tracked him down! A runner who had booked

Danny's trip had broken down under his interrogation and told him everything. 'How did you find me?' stammered Danny. Green coolly reminded him that he paid the runner's wages before explaining that the mechanics were working out if it was economically feasible to reconstruct the chassis of the stricken vehicle. In the end the car was a write-off. Danny would later lament that it could happen to anyone. 'It just happened to happen to me – and it just happened to be someone else's Ferrari,' were the words that he would repeat many times. Needless to say Danny lost the privilege of driving his boss's car.

Wrecking a Ferrari would not stop Danny from completing his apprenticeship. After he qualified as a trader he made the journey to Singapore in 1993 to work as a dealer for Carlsson's FCT. A year earlier I had made my second visit to the Asian financial hub. I had jumped at the chance of a return to SIMEX when Green said that he could arrange for me to spend some time back in Singapore with FCT. I was joined on the trip by my US Treasury bond trader Nigel 'Mad Dog' Bewick. The fact that I was great mates with Green, knew Carlsson, the big boss, and had supervised Danny when he was a blue button meant that Mad Dog and I were treated a bit like royalty during our stay.

SIMEX had made huge progress from the time of my last visit five years before. The boom in business at the exchange was largely a result of a mutual offset agreement on the Eurodollar contract with Chicago's CME. The agreement enabled dealers to net-out positions on both exchanges, leaving Liffe out in the cold. Volumes on SIMEX were growing each month at London's expense. This made me seriously consider setting up an operation in Singapore. But it soon became clear that the exchange no longer needed the help of experienced dealers from London. The fee holidays and other incentives which had been on the table when I last visited were not on offer anymore. If anything, we were now viewed as a potential competitive threat by the local trading community and no longer wanted. Without the credit limits which I would require to fund arbitrage dealing there were no incentives for us to come and trade.

I got the feeling that we were being frozen out. There were certainly no easy pickings over there anymore. It seemed like a wasted journey. My decision not to start up a Singapore venture would leave the playing field open for Danny when he arrived in the Asian financial hub next year.

A young Chinese clerk called Anthony had the job of making sure that we were entertained each evening. This turned out to be tough work for the young lad. He was a complete lightweight when it came to knocking back the bottles of Tiger beer and got absolutely slaughtered on the first couple of nights. When we saw how worse for wear he was on the morning of our third day we decided to give him a night off from the booze. Mad Dog thought that it would be a good idea if we tried some 'ethnic cuisine', rather than going to the posh downtown bars and restaurants where we had spent the previous couple of evenings. We took the train out to the suburbs which were inhabited only by local people. This made us feel a bit self-conscious being the only 'angmos' (red heads), the slang word used by Singaporeans to describe white foreigners who typically got burnt by the hot South East Asian sun.

Anthony led the way through the winding streets and took us to a busy market place. Amidst the hubbub was a crowded food court which housed about 100 rough-and-ready wooden dining tables. Here you would sit down to eat surrounded by about twenty stalls which displayed a variety of oriental food that never made it onto the menu at my local Chinese restaurant in Basildon. We asked Anthony to help us choose a selection of what was on offer. While culinary delights like fish heads were easy to identify, I had no idea what most of the stuff was. I quickly learnt that asking questions about what I was eating would not make me feel any more reassured. 'What are these Anthony,' I asked as I picked at what was on my plate. 'Hundred-year-old eggs,' was the brusque reply. He explained that the cooking process involved burying eggs in sawdust until they turned green before dipping them in ginger. Needless to say it was Mad Dog and I who were the ones looking ill the next morning and not Anthony.

When Danny arrived in Singapore he was one of the few British dealers on the island. He got to know Leeson during his first week of trading on SIMEX as a result of an incompetent broker at Barings. Danny was often shocked by the poor mathematical skills of some of the traders at Barings. Their dealing cards often did not add up correctly which left the bank frequently losing money in out trades. If Barings had employed experienced order fillers it could have saved a lot of money. But the management's greed led the bank to instead rely upon lowly-paid local workers that did not have the skill set required to do such a tough job. The subsequent losses in out trades would be the reason why Leeson set up the 88888 account in the first place. During Danny's first few days on the floor a Barings broker had made an errant trade with FCT which was set to cost the British bank tens of thousands of dollars. Danny spotted the mistake and offered to cancel a 45 lot futures contract with Barings after Leeson had intervened to confirm that his bank was at fault. Leeson appreciated this kind gesture and the pair became friends.

FCT became the biggest customer of Barings on SIMEX. Danny carried out arbitrage trades in Nikkei, Euroyen and Japanese Government Bond (JGB) futures, fulfilling a similar role to the one Green performed on the Liffe floor but in Singapore. These were the sort of trades Leeson was supposed to be doing as part of his role as General Manager at Barings Futures Singapore: low risk, cash intensive transactions which required margin payments at both SIMEX and the Tokyo Stock Exchange. Carlsson's FCT had $50 million tied up supporting Danny's arbitrage trading which consistently made the market for Leeson's dealing.

Danny did a good job of staying on top of business on the floor during his first five months while also keeping up with Leeson's ceaseless quest to explore Singapore's many nightspots. During this time he had no idea that Leeson was a married man! Being teetotal did not stop Danny from becoming a regular at places like Harry's Quayside Bar which became Leeson's favourite hangout. The rapport which the pair had fuelled their dealings with each other on the SIMEX floor. Danny's biggest win in the market would be on a trade with Barings. The British bank had bought the JGB futures up 20 ticks in the Tokyo lunch break while the Nikkei, Euroyen and currency (Dollar/Yen) had not budged. This left the market looking overbought. But most locals had sold to Barings on the way up and could not sell any more. When Danny returned from a coffee break he was amazed at how overbrought the market looked.

'Sold,' yelled Danny at Leeson.
'How many?' he asked.
'Your size big boy,' was Danny's quick riposte.
'1,062 lots,' retorted Leeson.

Danny almost cra**ed himself there and then. But his pride meant that he had to do the trade and everything he knew told him that it was a great trade. But he was left with an agonising three quarters of an hour wait until Tokyo opened after the lunch break. The open position was over $100,000 a tick. Danny called Carlsson in London at three o'clock in the morning to tell him what he had done. He thanked Danny for the call and wished him good luck. Five minutes later Carlsson was back on the phone questioning the trade. Perhaps the serenity of his night's sleep had been somewhat disturbed. After talking through the transaction again with Danny he finally agreed that it looked good value. The markets in Tokyo then opened lower, netting Danny a $1.3 million profit.

Danny and Leeson would take time to relax from the stresses of the SIMEX floor by going on holiday together. On one occasion the pair decided to take a golfing holiday in Indonesia. When completing the official forms for admission into the country, Danny answered 'briefly by Japan in 1943' to the question of occupation. Leeson had egged him on to do this and the pair thought that it was a pretty funny joke. The Indonesian authorities did not find it so amusing. Danny was frog marched away to a cell where he was strip searched and questioned for four and half hours. This was a terrifying experience for Danny and he vowed never to repeat the mistake that he had made. Leeson thought the whole episode was hilarious of course.

As everyone knows, Leeson did a first-class job of hiding his multi-million pound losses from those in his inner circle. Dealers on the floor never had any doubts that he was the star trader that he made himself out to be. This was just how he liked it. Supposedly winning trades in Singapore masked mounting losses in Tokyo. Even when he was getting blind drunk with Danny he never came close to saying a word about the desperate situation that he was in. Danny would later be very grateful that Leeson remained tight-lipped about what he was up to. Otherwise he would have been enormously tempted to use this knowledge to make a lot of money, which would have landed him in serious trouble. But he recalls that in hindsight Leeson did give hints of his troubles. Danny got caught in a bad position at the opening of a day's trading on one occasion which cost him money. When Leeson spotted Danny's bad luck he had a good laugh at his expense and was unfazed by the obligatory response of 'f**k off bastard.' Leeson just smiled and told him to lighten up. 'My morning is already ten times worse than yours. I wish I could swap places with you,' he said. Danny thought this was a strange remark to make at the time.

Danny had sensed that Leeson was in trouble but he had no idea of the scale of the losses which he had accumulated. A day before Leeson fled Singapore he confessed to Danny that he had been 'a naughty boy'. He did not mention the losses at Barings but he said that his life in Singapore was over. His job and bonus were gone. Danny went to Thailand for a short holiday after he drove Leeson to the airport. He returned home to find 99 messages on his answer machine. His best mate had just single-handedly destroyed the Queen of England's bank and the whole world knew about it.

I found out that Leeson was on the run before Danny and the general public. It would be on the night of 25 February 1995. I had been out with Green, Mad Dog and Clive Beauchamp to watch a fight at the New London Arena in Millwall which would have dreadful consequences for one of the fighters involved. The American Gerald McClellan was fighting Nigel Benn, a hard punching brawler from Ilford in Essex. Benn fought under the name the 'Dark Destroyer'. He was defending his WBC super middleweight world crown. I, like most people, thought that his title would be changing hands at the end of the night. McClellan had fought his way out of the ghetto to win the WBC middleweight world title and he epitomised the type of elite American middleweight that would come over to London and dish out a bad beating to the best that Britain had to offer.

Green had managed to get us seats about 10 rows back from the ring. This gave us a great view of the fight but Green was still not happy that a team of traders from Dean Witter had got one up on us, bagging ringside seats near a host of celebrities including Don King, Piers Morgan, who was the editor of the *Daily Mirror* newspaper, and a red-suited Frank Bruno. The British heavyweight boxer – who went on to win a version of the world crown before retiring to a life blighted by bouts of severe mental illness – would spend most of the contest on his feet loudly urging Benn on with a booming voice and pounding his fist on the ring canvas. When the opening bell rang it looked like we were going to be in for a quick night. McClellan walked through the Dark Destroyer's defences, banging him with a succession of punches which knocked Benn through the ropes and out of the ring. McClellan had to almost push the referee away as he went after Benn like a street fighter, looking to knock him out in the first round. Each punch which hammered into Benn sent him a message – that he had no business sharing a ring with the world champion in waiting. It looked just a matter of time before the referee would be forced to step in and stop the fight. But Benn stayed on his feet to last the round.

The bell rang for the beginning of round two and the whole arena took a collective in-take of breath. Benn came out as if the first round never happened – throwing right hands and winging hooks which made McClellan retreat on to the back foot for the first time. By now some of the people in front of us were jumping on to their seats to get a better view of the action. It would not be long before everyone near ringside was standing on their seats. I felt sorry for a well-to-do couple seated just behind us. You don't get too many short guys who make successful pit traders. We were all 6-foot plus and jumping up and down on our seats as if we were in the ring ourselves. From the second round onwards we noticed that McClellan was having difficulty keeping his gum shield in his mouth. He was also blinking a lot. We all assumed that these were the tell-tale signs of fatigue. McClellan specialised in taking his opponents out early. He was not used to being taken into the later rounds of a fight. More people in the baying crowd started to draw heart as the American slowed down. 'He's knackered. He's gone … He's gone.'

As the battle unfolded it became clear that we were witnessing no ordinary boxing match. Benn had already fought in two legendary battles of British boxing. He lost his first fight against the tragic Michael Watson and the second against Chris Eubank. Something deep within his psyche must have told him that there was no way that he was going to be a loser this time as he found himself deep down in the trenches of another ferocious battle. Relentlessly he came after McClellan, bobbing his head from side to side and offloading powerful hooks and upper cuts. This was total war. Benn would hit the canvas again in the eighth round before McClellan quit in the tenth round amid frenzied cheers inside the arena. I was among the 11,000-strong celebrating crowd which the sports writer Kevin Mitchell would describe as being 'drunk' on the 'violent conclusion' that we had witnessed. Then it would become clear that McClellan had been badly hurt. We watched as he was taken out of the ring on a stretcher.

Green invited us back to his Docklands apartment after the fight. As we were in Green's car driving back to his place the radio news had already reported that McClellan had been taken to hospital after a suspected blood clot had formed around his brain. The American would live the rest of his life blind and in a wheelchair. The mood in the car darkened. We all felt a bit emotionally drained and depleted when we arrived at Green's pad. My mind was still lost somewhere in the boxing ring that had hosted the spectacle of violence that we had all just witnessed. I poured myself a beer at the bar inside his flat and took in a panoramic display of the London's skyline lit up at night. I was not too interested in playing around with the surround-sound cinema, telescope, pool table and other boys' toys which Green had assembled in the apartment. I still could not resist making a joke about the telescope though. 'An interest in astronomy!' I exclaimed. I had to ask why he had kept his interest in the wonders of the uni-verse quiet for so long. Mad Dog couldn't resist asking whether the powerful viewfinder might not find itself looking at signs of life a bit closer to home, if there happened to be a few fit birds who liked to walk around with their kit off in the apartments nearby. The views must be just stunning, he quipped. As the evening wound down, Green got a call from Leeson's father. Nick had just gone missing. Nobody seemed to have a clue where he was. Had Green heard from him? I could tell speaking to Leeson's father had left Green concerned for his wellbeing. But I did not take in the significance of the telephone call at the time. I was still feeling a bit numb from the fight so everything seemed a bit surreal. I left the apartment not long after hearing the news about Leeson.

When I woke up the next morning the crisis at Barings was the leading story on the television news and Sunday newspapers. News reports were speculating about the size of the losses at the bank after a senior executive at Barings had apparently tipped off a Fleet Street newspaper the night before. I guessed that Leeson's dad may have already received a few calls from journalists before he called Green. The bank would be declared insolvent by the end of the day! When Nick was on the run he called Danny to express genuine shock at the figures that were being reported in connection with his rogue trading activities. He thought that the losses were less than £ 200 million and he did not believe for one minute that it would bring the bank down. As we now know, Leeson's losses were less than £ 325 million on the Friday when he fled the bank. It was only when the market discovered the positions that Barings had open that the bank went from a critical to terminal condition, losing another half a billion pounds in the frenzy of dealing on its corpse.

The fact that the whole world knew what Leeson had done made Danny a wanted man as well. The Singaporean authorities refused to believe that Danny was not involved in the rogue trading – given that he and Leeson were such good mates. The authorities took Danny's passport and put him under house arrest for several months without charge. He had to stump up $ 500,000 in bail money which he managed to do using his company's American Express credit card. SIMEX and the regulatory authorities in Singapore did not have a clue what Danny had been doing at the exchange. His trading strategy was a mystery to them and it was presumed that Danny was in cahoots with Leeson. SIMEX immediately cut Danny's positions. Unbeknown to the exchange this would cost Danny and FCT $1.7 million. Danny was left on a holding charge for intent to defraud which carried a prison sentence of between three and seven years. This did not concern Danny too much initially as he knew that he was innocent but after six months he became increasingly concerned. He was eventually released but instead of being dropped, the charges were suspended due to insufficient evidence. If the charges were dropped Danny would be able to sue the regulatory authorities for damages as a result of the trading losses which he suffered while he was under investigation. Carlsson was also a casualty in the Leeson affair. He had all his positions and assets frozen at FCT. Not being able to trade out of his financial positions took a huge toll on Carlsson's finances.

When the pair were left in the clear in Singapore, Danny came back to London to trade on Liffe. But solicitors representing Carlsson told him that it would be best if he traded for another member firm at the exchange until FCT had cleared everything up with London's Securities and Futures Association (SFA). This left Danny unemployed. Most firms would not touch him with a barge pole. There was a fear of being guilty by association with a man involved – albeit innocently – in the Leeson affair. I decided to hire Danny at Sussex Futures. I knew him well and thought he was a great guy so I had no problem with trusting him at my firm. I am sure Carlsson appreciated my decision to employ Danny which helped to get the trader's career back on track.

Not everyone was so confident in Danny's innocence. Lots of people in the market thought that he had made off with a fortune. When Danny started work back on the floor in London he was approached by the BTP pit's top boy who accused him of standing in his spot. Danny was not going to mess with the BTP king so he quickly moved down on to another step. Fifteen minutes later as the pit got busy Danny stepped back up near the BTP trader. This time the big man of the BTP pit whispered in his ear: 'I'll let you stand in my spot as you're the only trader in this pit who has as much money as me.' An embarrassed Danny did not know what to say. All he could do was step down again wishing that the BTP trader was really right.

His mate Nick would end the year with a six-and-a-half-year prison sentence in Singapore as a result of his fraudulent dealings. The collapse of Barings had a big impact on the Liffe market. Trading limits were reduced by the banks while the compliance and risk management departments of all the major financial institutions instigated thorough checks with the aim of ensuring that procedures would be put in place to prevent another Barings-style blow-up. This meant that we all suffered as a result of Leeson's actions.

While Danny worked for me he had a bit-part in the film *Rogue Trader*. He had wanted to play himself but the producers refused and he instead played an extra in the pit and had a role as technical adviser. You can see him in the scene where a Chinese trader working for Leeson has a fight in the pit – Danny plays the part of the guy he is scuffling with. I sometimes think about how things would have turned out if I had taken the decision to stay in Singapore. I would have traded through FCT and cleared through Barings. The chances are that I would have got to know Leeson very well. In the end I would never meet the most infamous futures and options trader of all time. But I feel that I do know Leeson by association in a strange way.

12

The Liffe Board

As I continued to develop the business of Sussex Futures on Liffe I felt confident that my decision to stay put in London and not move to a nascent market like Singapore was the right one. SIMEX might well have become the place to trade Eurodollars outside Chicago. But fighting daily battles in the pits for a living was no longer my life. I had given up being a full-time trader four and a half years ago in 1992. I was now a suit. Being a manager of a dealing firm which had about 70 employees involved quite a different skill set from trading in the markets. But I had taken to the role well and had made sure that I assembled a good team around me.

Ersser was proving himself to be a good floor manager. I would ask him for advice on important business matters and it was good to have someone so experienced around me. It was Ersser who first mentioned the possibility that I could stand as a candidate for the Liffe board. He thought it would be good for business if I became a director of the exchange. The more he kept mentioning the possibility, the more I began thinking about making a bid. I started to like the sound of the idea. But I would be up against the big banks and brokerage firms along with some of the most respected superstar traders on the floor. It would be a big embarrassment if I made a bid and nobody voted for me. To be eligible to vote in elections for the board, individuals had to own shares (trading permits). Given that the big corporate dealers on the exchange owned most of the shares, the odds of success seemed stacked against me. It appeared inevitable that the big banks would make sure that their best interests were represented by supporting one of their own. It would make no sense for them to vote for an independent guy like myself. Ersser was persistent in asking if I would stand though and when other people started to broach the subject I decided to throw my hat into the ring. This sort of thing was not uncharted territory given that I had already been elected to the committee of the Eurodollar pit. But the Liffe board was a big step up. Ersser assumed the unofficial role of my campaign manager. He told anybody who mattered what a good job I would do on the board. It was not long before a couple of highly respected ex-directors offered to propose and second me.

When the day of the election results came I felt very nervous. If everyone who promised to back me did so I would not be humiliated. Nevertheless, doubts started to creep into my mind. I wondered if the same people who had told me that I had their vote were saying the same thing to all the other candidates. Hell why did I let people talk me into this! It was not until late in the afternoon that the membership department of the board called to let me know the results. I picked up the telephone as the office fell silent. Everyone seemed to know what the call was about and my heart was beating fast. 'John, I am pleased to tell you that you have been successfully elected to the board of Liffe. Congratulations!' said the voice on the other end of the line. I gave my staff the thumbs up. Ersser jumped up and punched the air in delight. 'Yesssssss,' he yelled. Everybody looked so happy for me. I felt elated but as usual tried to do my best to look composed. The results were impressive. I had come third out of a dozen candidates. I was only beaten by two senior bankers working for UBS and JP Morgan and had won far more votes than I had expected. People must have thought that I knew what I was doing!

When I arrived for my first board meeting the only spare seat at the table was next to Lord Walker. 'John, I am Peter. Welcome to the board,' he said as I put my papers down on the table beside him. 'Thank you,' I replied before shaking his hand. I was too nervous to make conversation and I was a bit surprised he even knew who I was. There were a few other guys at the table who had worked their way up from the floor. Kyte and Steve Gaterell, the floor manager at Merrill Lynch were seated nearby. But the boardroom was still dominated by 'upstairs executives'. While I knew Furse from my days at Heinold I did not have much of an idea about who most of my new colleagues were. Nevertheless, I enjoyed the first meeting and was invited to serve on the commodities committee by Jack Wigglesworth, chairman of the board. After the meeting I felt that I had really achieved something in my life. I had come from a council estate in Basildon to sit as an elected member of the board of one of the City of London's leading financial institutions.

I soon settled into my new role. The other board members seemed to appreciate the pragmatic approach that I had to the business. If there was a subject being discussed that seemed unclear I would just say so. One board member said that I was like the child who said that the Emperor had no clothes. I would often say 'Please forgive me if I am being stupid. But this makes no sense to me ...' As often as not, everyone else would agree that they were also unclear on the point being discussed. Perhaps others were afraid of looking stupid. But I would never agree on something that I did not understand.

There were always a wide range of views exchanged at the table. But everybody was in agreement on one thing. The Deutsche Terminbörse (DTB) in Frankfurt was the near and pressing danger for the exchange, not the Chicago giants. The DTB had always been in Liffe's shadow but this was starting to change. As each year passed the threat it posed seemed to loom larger. By 1996 everybody seemed to be having restless nights over what Frankfurt would do next. The DTB was attacking our market share using the same military-style efficiency which had won its country victories against us on the football pitch. This time it was not a World Cup or European Championship at stake but the highly lucrative Euribor and Bund contracts which London had always had a stranglehold over. The

Germans saw Liffe's dependence on the open outcry dealing system as its Achilles heel. The DTB had developed a hi-tech electronic platform which it was using to pull business away from us. The Bund had accounted for a third of all Liffe's business but business was trickling to the DTB – by the summer of 1997 the Frankfurt-based exchange had captured a quarter of dealing in the contract. London trading firms were not going to let national pride get in the way of the bottom line. If the DTB offered a cheaper and more efficient dealing service it would not take long for them to switch their business to Frankfurt.

Kyte increasingly used board meetings to demand a reduction in the exchange fees at the exchange to counter the competitive threat from the DTB. Some members of the board were completely adamant that electronic computer-based trading would put Liffe out of business unless the exchange joined the technology-based arms race as well. The most ardent supporter of open outcry was Peter Regas. He still worked as a floor trader while serving on the board. The American did not have the appearance of a typical boardroom executive. He wore his long dark brown hair in a pony tail and had a beard. I doubt an Englishman could have got away with this look on the floor but people warmed to Regas and his American drawl. The man believed in the right to bear arms in his home country and he would often come out with quips that sounded like they had just been uttered in a Hollywood film. If he felt that an executive had made the wrong decision he would say: 'He has the keys to the vault but has no idea where the bank is.' Regas was not a big fan of the legal profession. He once told me that there are 'liars and there are lawyers' and it was his view that 'every lawyer is a God damn liar'. Regas would use board meetings to make impassioned arguments for the retention of open outcry. Once after a heated boardroom discussion I had a chat with Regas about the future of the exchange. 'You know my whole business depends on floor trading,' I told him. 'But when I think about where technology is going, sometimes I do have my doubts that in a decade from now we'll still be trading in the pits.' Regas looked me straight in the eye, weighing up the words that I had just spoken. 'John. I hear what you are saying. But I would sooner cut my d**k off than sell out to those bastards,' he said. Regas was never going to be a man for compromise. You were either with him or against him.

The very fact that the continued use of the open outcry system was in doubt showed just how stark the DTB threat was. I had visions of cunning German technocrats laughing at the drunken East End rabble running around the Liffe floor. Our enemies were no doubt trying to mastermind a state-of-the-art trading platform which would leave us all extinct. I doubt that any tears would have been shed by the DTB executives if this happened. Maybe the Teutonic plotters thought that the Liffe boys were the same hooligans which had gone on the rampage in Germany during the European Championships of 1988 – another English football disaster. In a few cases they would probably have been right! The Liffe board had not long ago discussed the possibility of moving to a much bigger exchange floor based in Spitalfields. Now we were contemplating building our own electronic trading platform. In the meantime, new technology was being introduced into the dealing pits to make trading more efficient. This included the introduction of headsets to speed up the trading process and the piloting of hand-held electronic trading cards.

Board meetings had gone from two-hour sessions to five or six-hour marathons. Things would get pretty heated during these lengthy debates. The non-executive chairman Jack Wigglesworth was too nice to have been in charge. He needed to be tougher. Daniel Hodson, the chief executive officer, would respond to this by trying to take control of meetings. Hodson had a similar manner to the London Mayor Boris Johnson, though his thin greying hair gave him a very different appearance. When he tried to take charge of meetings it would anger some of the other directors as it appeared to them that he was pushing his own agenda. He had long recognised that electronic trading was going to take over. But he did not have an easy time trying to convince the board of this. The mortal threat facing open outcry had not escaped the thoughts of dealers in the pits who depended on the system for their livelihoods. The death of the floor had been predicted before but this time traders were getting genuinely concerned for their jobs. I could feel this palpable sense of unease whenever I visited the floor. I would often get approached by worried traders who would say how good it was that 'one of us' was on the board. 'You will make sure that those w*****s upstairs don't sell us out won't you John?'

Dealers in the pits would discuss their hopes and fears for the future in meetings held in the exchange canteen. These would be organised by Regas who acted almost like a shop steward for the floor community. He would summon Hodson to these meetings along with prominent directors such as Kyte. I would always make sure that I turned up but these debates put me in a very difficult situation. I knew that there was no way of stopping the growth of electronic trading but in my heart I wanted open outcry to keep going in some form. The older traders had given 17 years of their life to making the market a success only to be told that they were now surplus to requirements. The meetings could feel like aggressive trade union conferences as some dealers vented their anger. The public school educated Hodson would stand in front of the baying dealers wearing the traditional City attire of a pinstripe suit and brightly polished shoes and tell them honestly where he thought the future of trading lay – which was on computer screens. This made him a very unpopular man on the floor but he showed good character in choosing to tell traders what he thought to their faces.

At one particularly rancorous meeting in the canteen, pit traders voiced anger over a recent change to dealing procedures. The exchange had decided that if an error had taken place in a floor transaction and the dealer had been lucky enough to trade out of it and take a profit, he would have to offer any money that he made to the customer. But if it turned out to be a losing trade he would have to carry the loss. The rationale behind the rule change was that it would provide desk traders with a guarantee of fairness and parity with the floor. This was a well-meant but misguided tinkering with floor rules. As usual, Regas came out with an amusing statement which he felt summed up the pit trader's plight. 'It is like being the only guy in the room holding a knife in a gun fight,' he said. Everybody just burst out laughing.

The DTB threat was not going to go away. The tipping point in the balance of power for Bund trading took place in the Autumn of 1997 when Liffe's monthly share of dealing in the contract fell from 4,802.534 in October to 2,636.995 in November. These monthly falls prompted frantic boardroom meetings which went on late into the night as we agonised over how to respond to the threat. We decided to offer a fee-free holiday for dealing the Bund. This achieved nothing. The DTB continued to eat away at our market share. The feedback from market participants and other directors on the board was that desk traders preferred to deal on-screen – which meant trading on the DTB. So-called click-and-trade dealing was more transparent, cheaper and quicker than open outcry. By April 1998, Liffe's monthly share in Bund trading had fallen to 1,556.976. Liffe was now a minor player in a contract which had been its most traded product. By the end of the year, Liffe's share in dealing of the Bund would fall from 70% to zero.

An emergency board meeting was held at Down Hall country house in Hertfordshire to decide if the exchange was going to have its own electronic platform. The board was split almost fifty-fifty on the issue. I had to vote for the retention of open outcry – my business depended on it at the time and I was not about to betray the dealers in the pits. When I parked my car for the meeting I could not help but notice the fine collection of vehicles in the car park which showed just how wealthy the members of the board were. But nobody could beat Richard Berliand, head of futures at JP Morgan, for an ostentatious display of wealth. He chose to arrive by helicopter. Kyte was the only director not to attend as he was on holiday. Both sides argued their case strongly. Regas used the occasion to make another impromptu speech on why we had to keep the floor. This would be to no avail. The matter was settled by the votes of the chairman Wigglesworth and Daniel Hodson, the chief executive officer (CEO), who both favoured the introduction of an electronic platform.

When I got in my car and started the long two-hour drive home I felt numb. At first I felt like I did not have a future in the industry any more. The decision was a killer blow for my business at the time. But by the end of my drive home I had accepted the board's decision.

It had been the right one and needed to be embraced. Now I had to face up to the new challenges which technology had brought to the industry.

Kyte stood up and announced his resignation at the next board meeting. He told us all that our heads had been stuck up our own arses for far too long. Kyte told us that he was going to trade on the DTB. His resignation from the board was front-page news in the *Financial Times* the next day. He used the story to announce that he would open a new electronic trading room next month. Kyte knew how to use the media. He really looked like a man with a vision of what the new trading technology could do. 'The chairman and chief executive [of Liffe] remind me of the captain and chief engineer on the Titanic thinking their ship is unsinkable. Gentlemen, the iceberg is just around the corner,' Kyte was quoted as saying in the press.

Now the rest of us had to face the tough decisions which needed to be made. My God what had I let myself in for! I had a good sense of what the financial markets in London would look like in a few years' time – and it did not involve dealers running around a floor with pieces of paper in their hands. This was a devastating realisation. Not just for my own business but for the traders on the floor for whom I felt like a spokesman. Many would lose their jobs. The decision to build our own electronic platform was sealed. The plan was to initially develop a hybrid model in which customers of the exchange had the choice of trading either electronically or in the pits. I now had the unenviable task of explaining to my people why the board had voted against open outcry trading. This was not easy. But people are not stupid – especially guys who make a living in the cut-throat futures business – and most dealers seemed to understand. In an electronic age we had to give customers a choice of how they wanted to trade. Most did not give me a hard time. It was pretty clear that my decision was not based on self-interest given that my firm was a floor brokerage business. I hoped in my heart that the floor would be able to continue for a few more years.

Hanbury Manor, a golf and country club in Hertfordshire, was the venue for another away-day meeting of the board. We needed to make big decisions fast. A new share structure was the first thing that had to be agreed. The key for success would be to make it widely available. There would not be a requirement for trading permits on an electronic market which meant that all customers would be able to obtain access to the market without needing to trade via permit holders. On the floor dealers needed a certain type of share to trade particular contracts. For example, an A share allowed a dealer to trade in any pit on the floor and carried 20 votes. A C share allowed a dealer to trade in all the pits except the gilt and short sterling pits and carried five votes. An E share entitled dealers to trade only in the BTP pit. Eurolira and the European Currency Unit (ECU) carried just one vote respectively. The problem was that the value of each share did not accurately represent its voting power. A shares cost £250,000 which meant that a C share should have been worth £62,000 but these shares were trading at £150,000. E shares should have been valued at £12,500 but these securities were trading at £80,000. The prices reflected the trading rights not the share value. Ian Nash, the company secretary of the board, explained that for legal reasons the trading permits had to be converted into shares for the new electronic market. The conversion would be based upon the voting rights which the shares entitled their owner to and not their current market value. Quite a few members of the board argued that this was grossly unfair. This was a major blow for me personally. I knew that once the announcement of the new share structure was made the value of the C and E shares would collapse. But insider trading laws prevented me from selling. First my livelihood had been taken away from me and now the value of my investments were about to plummet in value. I owned four C shares and nine E shares. The decision to restructure the value of shares at the exchange was about to cost me almost £1 million! I did not find this too amusing – but I still voted in favour of the new share structure. Unfortunately, we had little choice but to do this.

The next big decision to be made was whether to build our own system or hire a specialist firm to do the job. We invited MATIF, the Paris-based bourse, to pitch for the job. The French sent over a team of 20 to make a presentation in front of the executive technology director Simon Orebi Gann. The chairman chose me to join Orebi

Gann's team to hear the presentation. The French argued their case well in the morning but by the afternoon Orebi Gann's team had picked some holes in their plan. Our guys felt that they could do a better job themselves and I believed them. We made a recommendation to the board that we build our own system. Orebi Gann's team was very confident that a far superior system to the platform used by the DTB could be built in just one year. The board gave this plan the thumbs up. Nobody else was close to delivering a system that could trade short-end contracts as efficiently in the pits in the short term. The open outcry system still had a significant advantage over electronic dealing when it came to more complex transactions such as the Euromark, which was now the most popular traded contract on Liffe. The damage had already been done with the Bund contract so we had little to lose.

The new electronic platform was to be called Liffe Connect. A committee titled the Automated Markets Advisory Group (AMAG) was quickly assembled to guide the technology team on what trading functions the new system should have. Steve Hills, an options market specialist, was appointed the chairman and I was made his deputy. We were joined by 10 senior market professionals and would answer any questions that the developers had and make recommendations on what needed to be done. It was an efficient and dynamic group and the development of trading technology that has since proved very successful – such as Liffe's pro-rata algorithm – was agreed at these meetings.

My role on the board also involved serving on a sub-committee which advised those involved in the Liffe Connect project on the development of the platform. We discussed areas such as the open architecture software for the front-end of the platform, which enabled technology companies to plug into the exchange and do business for their banking customers. I also served on the chairman select committee which had to decide on an executive chairman. This committee included Sir Michael Jenkins and Sir Brian Williamson and our task was to find the right person for the job. Furse was among the candidates that we interviewed. Having known her all those years ago when she was a broker at Heinold, I may have found it difficult to assess Furse objectively next to such high-profile candidates in the industry. She would go on to do a good job as chief executive at the London Stock Exchange, a business which has also learned about the competitive perils that new technology can bring. We needed to find somebody who could appreciate the difficult position we were in, with the intuition needed to guide us on the right path as technology took the industry into a new era. After weeks of intensive interviews and meetings with head hunters an outstanding candidate had still not emerged. One evening Sir Michael Jenkins called me at home and hinted that he might be able to get Brian Williamson to take on the role. He asked if I would support the appointment. I agreed and within days he was appointed the first executive chairman at Liffe.

After the appointment of Williamson, I felt that my work on the board had been done. The Liffe Connect electronic platform was launched on time on 30 November 1998 for equity options. A process then followed in which the exchange's other financial contracts were transferred from floor to screen. It felt like Liffe was now on the right path. I was also not spending enough time with my family. In the first half of 1999 I tendered my resignation from the board. Williamson said that he did not want to lose me but he accepted my decision and I agreed to stay on for another six months on the board's steering group for Liffe Connect. The fallout from the decisions which the board took had made a major impact on the lives of the hard-working people that I had known for years on the floor. The Liffe Connect platform would support a new generation of technology-savvy traders in London. But for the old generation, its introduction would mark the beginning of the end.

13

My Rogue Trader

Liffe had made its decision to join the technology arms race. Now I had to make a decision of my own. Did I enter the fray in a new electronic age or walk away into retirement? It was not as if I needed the money. I was 40 – ancient enough for a player in the capital markets – and had earned enough to have a prosperous life outside of finance. But the hunger was still there. At the time I thought it was my staff that persuaded me to set up a new office and build a screen-based trading venture. But the truth was that I needed to prove it to myself. I needed to show beyond doubt that I was not just a lucky guy whose career success had been built on being in the right place at the right time.

The writing was on the wall for open outcry as the nineties drew to a close. Banks started to close their floor operations which left them needing a floor-based broker. Many banks asked my firm to execute their orders in the pits. This led to an explosion of business at Sussex Futures in the first half of 1999. A lot of the traders and brokers who had lost their jobs on the floor came to me and promised to use my firm for their execution business. Dealers also made deposits to trade on my new electronic platform. The new offices were located near the heart of the City at 4 St Dunstan's Hill which is situated between Eastcheap and Lower Thames Street. This is just 400 yards away from the Monument, one of the square mile's famous landmarks.

I had acquired the office space, which included a 4,000 square foot dealing room, from Refco, a major futures broker in the US. I had also agreed to purchase £500,000 of IT equipment which included servers, PCs, and telephone systems along with furniture for a knock-down price of £100,000. The equipment had previously been used by a failed trading group before being left idle in a disaster recovery site. It was perfect for our needs housing 50 dealing desks. My own office was quite stark. I never bothered to decorate it, save for a couple of framed photographs of the Liffe floor. I would sit with my back to the window, facing a glass wall through which I could observe my team of brokers and traders who toiled away in front of 21-inch screens.

The new trading room was virtually full within a matter of months and the mushrooming levels of business going through my books was putting a strain on my clearer, Royal Bank of Scotland. RBS told me that it could no longer provide statements and administration because the amount of business was too high. This was just too much for them. Sussex Futures was now trading 10 times more business than RBS. Sussex Futures jumped from 19 to number 3 in the league for pit-traded volumes. I was the owner of the biggest independent broker in Europe! What a shame this could not last. To cope with the high dealing volumes I purchased a fully automated back office system from a French software company for about £250,000. RBS agreed to finance it over a period of five years. This all seemed like good business to me. I felt that once we had the system bedded down we would be independent. If dealing volumes held up I planned to raise the £2 million needed to set up my own clearing system.

I had recruited David Stuart, a Liffe director and senior manager at ING, the Dutch investment bank, to oversee the new back office operation and act as my deputy. Marc Kingston, a senior Liffe admin-istrator, became my compliance officer while Mark Penny, the dark-haired older brother of my order filler Keith, got the floor manager's job. He had worked in this role before at Lloyds Bank and I had served alongside him on Liffe's AMAG committee. Penny was at home with technology and perfectly suited to the new era of electronic trading. Ersser and Moffat, on the other hand, had reached their late forties and early fifties respectively and were a little technophobic. These guys were not going to make the transition to the screens when floor trading died.

The Chinese proverb about living in interesting times just about summed up my predicament. I was working flat out and making a lot of deals. It was at this time that a quietly spoken man named Stephen Humphries turned up at my office one day and asked if he could trade. He said he had £20,000 of equity which he wanted to lodge with Sussex Futures in order to trade gilts on my new electronic platform. He had apparently traded on the floor before but I did not recognise him. The son of an electrician, his short dark brown hair and medium build did not distinguish him from the hundreds of other dealers who worked in the dealing pits.

When I interviewed Humphries he came across well. He seemed knowledgeable about the business and gave all the right answers to my questions. I was keen to focus my energies on building my new business rather than recruiting staff and by appointing Humphries I had been able to fill my trading room without even having to publish an advertisement. This seemed great! Before he came on board I asked some of my traders if they knew Humphries. He had been seen dealing in the pits and nobody knew of any reason why I should not hire him. He passed a compliance check and had never fallen into problems with securities regulators in the past. A credit reference check did not disclose that he had any debts. He signed the customer agreement paperwork and we shook hands on the deal.

When Humphries started work he was the quiet man who sits in the corner. He did nothing which raised any concerns at all in his first couple of months. During this time he stayed well within his trading limits and never had more than 20 or 30 lots on. He earned £5,000 and never lost or made more than £1,000 in a single day. This would all change on 6 August 1999 when the US unemployment figures were published. I had taken a day off to deal with the builders at my home. I had recently moved out of a £1 million house on the river in Maidenhead and moved back to a modest home in Basildon which needed some work doing to it. Humphries had already broken his trading limits in the morning but it had not been picked up. It was not a serious breach.

The new back office system had gone live four days earlier and we had been suffering a lot of technical teething problems. These troubles were exacerbated by a glitch in the software at the front-end of the system which made the trading screens freeze when a dealer neared his trading limits. To solve this problem I had turned off the position limits and let the clerks check dealing positions using the Trade Registration System (TRS). This is how trades had been checked for the past 17 years when dealing had been done on the floor. During this time I never had a serious breach where a dealer broke his trading limits. Nevertheless, I knew depending on the TRS system for screen-based trading was far from ideal but it is not unusual for technical problems to occur when new technology is introduced. My reliance on the old system would only be for a month while the software was upgraded.

I had arranged for three clerks in the office to check the positions and profit and loss of my screen-based dealers. The new back office system would also get the trade information so the positions could be double-checked. We were in the holiday month of August and there were less staff around than usual. Many of the clerks on the floor knew that it would probably be time to start looking for a new career the following month after the trading of financial futures on the floor came to an end. The whole financial system could collapse as far as these guys were concerned. A booked holiday was going to be taken. What was I going to do, fire them? When a clerk called in sick the senior clerk summoned a clerical worker in the office to the dealing floor. We now had just two clerks checking the positions of traders in the office and one had asked to leave early as he was going on holiday that evening. I was about to be caught in a perfect storm as Humphries scanned the US unemployment figures and prepared to unleash hell.

A mass of trades hit our system half an hour after the figures from America had been released. Humphries was building up an enormous position. A clerk immediately went round to see him to ask what was going on. He found a contrite Humphries who said that he had over-traded and was in the process of closing his trading positions. He claimed to have nothing like the large number of open trades which the clerk had spotted. Ten minutes later more trades were hitting the system – adding to the position which Humphries had taken in the market – not closing it out. David Stuart, my deputy, was told what was happening. He then checked the positions on the new back office system. To his astonishment, the system revealed that we were long by hundreds of lots. He thought this surely had to be a mistake. The system was new and the positions were so large it looked like a technology malfunction.

When Stuart confronted Humphries he claimed that there must be some sort of a mistake in the back office system. He was not long over 500 lots! He had never traded more than 20 lots before this so his claim seemed believable. Stuart ordered him to close out his open positions immediately while he checked the back office system – which revealed that even more buy orders were raining into the market. Humphries was not exiting his positions – he was continuing to add to them! Stuart and my back office support staff could not believe what they were seeing. He double-checked the trades with TRS and it was agreed that Humphries had purchased 1,129 lots of gilts. This was the biggest position in the market. In a state of panic my men ran to confront Humphries. An empty desk awaited them. The trader sitting next to his desk said he had casually walked out of the office a couple of minutes ago for a cigarette break. But Humphries was nowhere to be seen. He had decided to flee. Penny logged into his PC to check the trades corresponded with the TRS and the back office system. It had taken Humphries just 43 minutes to make his disastrous bets on the government bond markets.

A quiet day in the sunshine of my back garden was about to come to an abrupt end. 'John, there is someone on the telephone for you. He says it is urgent,' shouted my wife as I was talking to some of the builders. 'John, we have a serious problem,' were the words that greeted me. My initial thoughts were that we must have a big out trade on the floor. 'We are long 1,129 gilts,' explained Penny. I took a double-take on this news. What the hell had happened! He told me that he was sure the numbers were correct and he estimated that we were looking at a loss of between £700,000 and £800,000. The market was very thin. It would be a big problem trading out of such a large position without further moving the market against us.

I might have long ago become a suit but my whole livelihood now once again depended on my skills as a trader. If the market moved further against these positions I could lose everything I owned. Trying to clear these thoughts from my mind was not easy as I told Penny I was going to trade my way of these positions. 'Okay, tell me what the prices are and I will see if I can get us out of this mess,' I said. I desperately needed the market to go up or at least not fall any further as this could cost millions. Running these types of positions overnight was a risk that just could not be taken. The first rule of trading is to never run errors. These positions had to be exited right away. The problem was the market was only bid on 30 lots and if I sold all the bids beneath the market the losses would spiral to more than £1.5 million. I had to make sure I did not spook the market. This meant that I never showed an offer. I would force the other sellers in the market to hit the bids, thereby driving the market down. I had to be really smart about how I sold. I waited for the bid to build up before selling and backing off again. This was the most nerve-racking 45 minutes of my life. Like a professional poker player who has to make sure that no one else has a clue what is in his hand I had to delicately offload the ruinous positions without letting any would-be predators smell blood. This I managed to do and I only moved the price six ticks. I did a bloody good job even if I say so myself!

I could breathe a sigh of relief. I did not have to worry about bankruptcy and the repossession of the family home which I was standing in. Now I had a business on the brink of collapse to sort out. Still unshaven and dressed in shorts and T-shirt I got on a train to Fenchurch Street and was there in three quarters of an hour. The Securities and Futures Authority (SFA) and RBS, our clearing firm, had been told about what had happened. When I arrived at the office about 30 or 40 traders from the floor were gathered around waiting for me. There was an old saying in finance: 'Good news travels fast, but bad news travels instantly.' Word of the rogue trading incident had quickly got out. The traders that had dealing accounts with my firm were terrified that their money was lost. The rumours were that I was sitting on a loss of several million pounds. Many of these guys were going to be out of work the next month. Being paid off would not be enough for them. The money held with my firm was needed to build a new future. One panic-stricken trader had abused and threatened a senior member of my staff and forced him to write out a cheque for his account balance. People can get very nasty indeed when sums of money like this can be lost. I thought that I could be facing a mob.

When I arrived the place fell silent. I stood outside my glass-walled office which overlooked the trading floor and explained to my staff what had happened. I confirmed that the loss was £743,000 and I would personally guarantee all their funds. If anybody needed a cheque I would write it out for them now. At that point someone shouted 'That's good enough for me John. I don't need a cheque – see you on Monday.' A spontaneous round of applause erupted after-wards and everybody started to leave. Not one person asked for a cheque. This show of faith brought a tear to my eye. Thank you for trusting me I thought. But your word is your bond when you are brought up on open outcry trading.

RBS and the SFA would not be as sympathetic. An official from the SFA and Will Lawton, head of futures at RBS were waiting for me. I had to give them hard documentary proof that Sussex Futures was still solvent and ready to open for business on Monday. My compliance officer managed to find a telephone number for Humphries and I spoke to him later that evening. He told me that he was really sorry for what he had done and was ready to go to jail. He seemed genuinely upset and remorseful. I knew yelling and shouting at him down the phone would not do any good. My mind was already focused on finding the best way of dealing with the situation. I asked if there was anything else that we did not know about and he assured me that there was not. I did not leave the office to go home until midnight.

A feeling of dread consumed me from the moment I opened my eyes the next morning. I had not just had a terrible dream. A trusted employee had just decided to gamble on the financial markets using my livelihood as the collateral. Now I had to try and pick up the pieces. Beauchamp, a trusted back office support clerk, and Diane Lingham, my accountant, spent the whole weekend trying to sort out the mess and find the information which RBS and the financial regulators required. Diane worked flat-out for 30 hours solid. The explosion of brokerage business which we had recently enjoyed and the fact that RBS no longer produced our statements made her task even more difficult. The technical problems we had experienced with the new electronic platform did not help either. These had to be put right before the firm could trade again. We were finally able to convince both RBS and the SFA that we were solvent which meant that we had permission to open our doors for trading on Monday morning. I hoped that everything would get back to normal in a few days. I would have just lost £743,000! Boy was I wrong!

I picked up a copy of the *Financial Times* to find that I was now front page news. The other broadsheets were all over the story as well. The headlines said it all. 'Liffe trader loses £750,000 on futures bet, Computer failure allows trader to lose £1.5m ...' To make matters worse, some newspapers quoted figures which were well wide of the market, estimating my losses at £1.5 million. I had experience of dealing with the financial press and have always found the reporting to be generally fair. I know journalists have a story to write. Dealing with this sort of media scrutiny was something else though. My telephone would not stop ringing. I did my best to set the record straight and found the majority of what was written to be accurate. This was not good publicity but it seemed manageable.

When the *Daily Mail* called I started to lose control of the situation. I told a reporter who had camped outside my offices that I had no comment. But the *Mail* was persistent in wanting me to talk and I eventually decided that it would probably be in my best interests to give the newspaper some more commentary. My sense of unease was not helped when my story was splashed across page seven the next day. 'Trader loses £743,000 in 43 minutes,' proclaimed the headline. The newspaper suggested that the incident echoed the Nick Leeson rogue trading scandal. The image of barrow boys once again going wild on the financial markets was not good for business. At least things could not get any worse, I thought … I was wrong.

Humphries had sold his story to the *Mail on Sunday*. The headline screamed: 'They all take risks like me says rogue trader who lost £750,000.' His words were printed next to a photograph of him wearing dark sunglasses with a wide grin on his face while speaking on a mobile. 'I have been made a scapegoat,' he claimed. 'This is happening all the time. I have been trading for two or three years and I can tell you I am one of many. This sort of risk taking is rife.' A reader of the *Mail on Sunday* could have been forgiven for thinking that Liffe dealers were working in one big casino. What a load of rubbish! He would have had no chance of trading in this way on the floor. He would have been spotted in no time and stopped. But a glitch in the software programme had enabled him to get away with his crazed bets on the futures market.

It turned out that Humphries had borrowed his £20,000 dealing deposit. This had been his last chance to make it as a trader. Having lost between £10,000 and £12,000 just before the US unemployment statistics had been published he chose to carry on buying, despite the bearish figure. Within minutes he was £25,000 down. Like a drunk at the roulette table he reasoned that he had nothing to lose. The absence of trading limits meant that he could bet (my) house on a rally in the market. This was never going to happen of course. Every time he purchased more gilt contracts his losing position grew larger. Lies to my staff let him dig a deeper hole. Like a gambler who keeps doubling up he had been desperate to win back his losses. When the game was up he fled. Humphries never even knew how much money he had lost. What did it matter to him? He owned nothing and could never repay a penny. I knew spending time thinking about him was of no use to me. I had to live with the consequences of his actions which left me in a battle to survive. Saving my business was not going to be easy. I converted loans I had given the company to permanent share capital and made a fresh loan of £250,000 from my savings to replace the monies lost. Job done, I thought. I should have been so lucky!

I tried to keep RBS happy by offering my Liffe shares as collateral. The bank refused and demanded cash instead. This forced me to accept a £5-a-share offer for the 50,000 shares which I owned from Spear, Leeds & Kellogg, the specialist trading company. I agreed to keep RBS happy and boost the balance sheet. A couple of years earlier the shares had been trading at £30. Pan-European exchange Euronext would pay £18.25 a share when it took over Liffe two years later. I did not have to spend too much time doing the maths to see how badly I had lost out. But I had no choice and losing a fortune on my Liffe shares was far from my main worry.

I was about to get first-hand experience of the icy calculation of the banks now I had fallen on hard times. RBS's head of treasury decided that I would have to lodge another £500,000 to guarantee my firm's business going forward. The SFA launched a full-blown investigation into Sussex Futures. I was now on the brink of collapse, according to reports in the financial media. The RBS demands meant that I had to pump more of my savings into the business but my wife was reluctant for me to do this. She knew we could lose everything if an event like this ever happened again. All I could do was reassure her that I had plenty of offers from financial institutions which wanted to invest in my business.

Spear Leeds proposed turning Sussex Futures into a joint venture with the US firm owning half of the company. I had a good relationship with their management and felt that I could do business with them. But time was not on our side. Spear Leeds was unable to move quickly. It would be two weeks before it could send a team over to Sussex Futures to do due diligence on the firm and a further couple of months before a firm offer could be made. I needed the money straight away but I had not found any of the other offers appealing. GHF had offered to merge both businesses on balance sheet value, which did not put me in a good position. GHF had a lot more cash than me – especially after I had lost £743,000 while my firm had a lot more business on its books. I could not accept that deal.

John Vowell, a venture capitalist, introduced me to John Gunn, a famous name in the City and former head of Exco and British Commonwealth. We had a meeting in my office. Vowell was in his mid-thirties and slightly overweight. He had the aura of a self-made man who had been a successful entrepreneur. Gunn was a bit over-weight and in his late fifties with dark thinning hair. Gunn told me that his daughter had worked on the exchange floor and that he knew all about me. How much money did I need, he asked in a blunt self-assured voice. '£600,000 should cover it,' I said. I was starting to like how this man did business. 'You've got it. John Vowell will get my solicitors to draw up the papers. Nice to have met you,' he replied. Then he left my office. He had not even asked to check my books. He just wanted to sort out our short-term problem and then sell the shares back for a quick profit when things got back to normal. He wanted to take a quarter of the business's profits in return for the risk that he was taking as he could lose all his money if the funding did not turn things around. This worked fine for me.

I had carried on talks with Spear Leeds but things were not moving fast. A couple of weeks later David Wenman came to see me. He was one of the most respected people in the City. He made his money after he sold his shares in O'Connor & Partners, the US broker, to Union Bank of Switzerland (UBS), the Swiss banking giant. After managing O'Connor's dealing room for years he had retired to pursue a passion for classic cars. I got to know him after Liffe enticed him back to the City with a place on the board to help with the introduction of Liffe Connect.

When Wenman came to see me he said that he would be willing to buy out John Gunn and Hugh Morgan. He wanted to become my partner splitting the business fifty-fifty and he was willing to pay £1 million to make this happen. This effectively meant that he would be paying £750,000 into the business that I had lost and compensating John Gunn very generously for his quick turn and buying Hugh Morgan's 10%. I would go from owning 90% of the share capital to 50%. But I would have Wenman as a partner. This sounded good enough to me and I agreed. I told Spear Leeds that I could not wait forever. I had done a deal with Wenman. The US trading firm said it understood and knew Wenman well enough to understand why I had made this decision.

I received another boost when I recruited Marc Bailey as managing director. We had both served on the Liffe board, though not at the same time. I had known him from my days on the floor when he had carved out a successful career as a local before becoming head of futures at JP Morgan. I was prepared to let him become managing director while I would be chairman. I felt having Wenman and Bailey on board would give our management team a real boost. I was also humbled by the support I received from the trading community. Carlsson and Green were among those offering support. Even some of my traders offered to lend me sums of money, which made me feel quite emotional. The Liffe board's steering committee refused to accept my offer of resignation.

Then I was hit with another bombshell. RBS decided out of the blue that it did not understand or value my business anymore. I was given one month to find a new clearer. RBS had enjoyed 10 years of making good money from Sussex Futures. But when I needed the bank the most it had dumped me at the drop of a hat. I was gutted. I later heard that the bank's futures department had proposed buying out my firm only to lose by one vote at board level. This would have been of no consolation. I was out of business the next month unless I found a new clearer. The GHF offer was still on the table. But I needed a big-name clearer. Once again, a friend would try to come to my rescue in these difficult times. Paul Lewis, the head of global futures at Deutsche Bank, agreed to clear our business. It looked like I was saved.

I could see a glimmer of hope at the end of the tunnel. This would not last long though. Liffe announced the closure of more dealing pits at the end of August. This meant 50 of my staff and traders would lose their jobs and want to be paid the money Sussex Futures owed them. The only problem was I still had £2.3 million in unpaid brokerage fees outstanding on my books. I should have made them wait for the money until I collected this debt. But there were still rumours swirling around that I was in trouble. My refusal to pay out immediately could give weight to these rumours. So I decided to pay everyone who asked for their money. This was a big mistake.

Deutsche Bank had only been on board as my clearer for one month before the German investment bank chose to change the terms of the deal. After discovering that I had done even more futures business than the bank itself, Deutsche Bank's compliance department decided that I should lay down £5 million as a guarantee and not the £500,000 I had lodged. I did not have a chance in hell of raising another £1 million let alone £5 million! This left me with just one month to find another clearer. I was finished. There was no way that the business could survive a move to another clearing house. We were already being looked upon as a credit risk by many market participants. I was quickly running out of options.

During this time I was approached by the police who wanted to prosecute Humphries. I agreed to cooperate. The police were following a directive to punish white collar crime in the City and this was a better course of justice than the other offers I had received. I had been told by a couple of traders that I only had to say the word and Humphries would be 'taken care of'. I told them that they were mad and on no circumstances should he be touched.

I agreed to close my office and switch my operations to GHF. I had decided to deposit £1.2 million in cash into the new business when my affairs were sorted out. This consisted of my £600,000 and £600,000 from Wenman. We would obtain 33% of the shares, of which I would own just 16.5% of the new company. Three months earlier I would never have considered this deal. But this was the best I could get now. Surely this was the end and I could just get back to trading and broking futures contracts. Marc Bailey resigned as managing director. This was a real disappointment as I am sure he would have been a success but I understood why he had decided to go. It had not been what he had signed up for. David Stuart was the next to leave. He probably would not have played a part in the new venture anyway but things got even more precarious when many of my traders and brokers refused to move offices. They liked it where they were and did not want to move. A place like GHF was not where many of my dealers wanted to be – this is why they had joined Sussex Futures in the first place. GHF insisted that all my staff had to move into their office within a couple of months. The newly merged company could not supervise the business from two locations and pay for a second office when thousands of square feet of office space were lying vacant.

I eventually persuaded about half of my staff to move. Those who stayed managed to get ADM, a brokerage firm, to hire them in my old office. I agreed. At least I could transfer the lease over. I received £40,000 back for the equipment which I had paid £100,000 for a year ago. The SFA was still on my back as well. It was costing me a fortune in legal fees and bills to accountants to keep the financial regulators and banks happy. Liffe added to my woes by carrying out its own investigation into the Humphries affair. I was fighting my corner as best as I could. But every time I tried to manoeuvre my way out of trouble I seemed to walk head on into another blow. These were extremely stressful times. I had lost a stone in weight. This showed as I have never been fat. Luckily I had the support of a good friend in Wenman. He never complained once.

The back office system I had bought was identical to the system used by GHF and consequently we had no further use for it and it was not resaleable. I told the French company about the difficulties I was having and hoped for a sympathetic ear. I got a solicitor's letter instead. No, I would not be allowed to terminate the agreement early. I had to pay the full amount or face legal action. My protests fell on deaf ears. The agreement I had signed was watertight. I had to pay the full £250,000 and RBS had withdrawn its funding offer. How nice of them! I ended up having to pay the full amount for two months' use. I wondered if things could get any worse. It would not take long to find out that they could.

Collecting the brokerage fees for July, August and September was tough work. The credit collection process was not helped by a mountain of paperwork which had accumulated while we were introducing the new systems. A lot of the brokers who had executed the business had been paid off and left while many of the staff that processed the transactions had also left. There were disputes over the agreed rates of commission. It took months of hard work to get £2 million of the £2.3 million we were owed and I had to write off another £300,000.

I was swimming in deep water and on the brink of financial collapse and – unbeknown to me – some of my brokers were on the verge of going to the wall as well. A broker who owed me £80,000 wiped the slate clean by declaring himself bankrupt. I would not get a penny. Another trader who owed £10,000 walked into my office, wrote me a cheque and made sure to look me straight in the eye as he thanked me for everything that I had done for him. The cheque bounced and he disappeared. I would discover that he had done a runner from the tax man as well and had escaped to somewhere in South East Asia. This type of behaviour would never have happened before the floor closed. If you had a debt you worked it off or you lost your registration. A bankrupt could not work in the industry and no other member of the exchange would employ a trader if he owed another member any money. This meant that all debts were honoured. But this code had broken when the floor closed. People were leaving the industry and looking after number one. While I had been blind-sided by the disaster which Humphries had unleashed some had seen an opportunity to profit from my misery.

It would take over a year to sort everything out. Liffe's investigation concluded that we were short-staffed on the day but no exchange rules had been broken. The bureaucrats at the SFA took a less sympathetic view. Perhaps the watchdog felt that it had to justify the thousands of pounds of taxpayers' money which had been spent during its investigation. We were reprimanded over my firm's failure to have sufficient controls in place and staff around on the day of the incident. I paid £5,500 while David Stuart also had to pay £2,750 in costs. The SFA case was reported across the national newspapers again, to add insult to injury. While the regulator recognised that there were mitigating circumstances I just accepted the decision. The whole thing had gone on for more than a year and a half by now and I was completely drained. David Stuart's only crime had been to serve as my deputy. Now a black mark had been left on his career. It all seemed so unfair and my lawyers had urged me to fight the unjust ruling. But I simply did not have the stomach for the fight anymore.

After spending months preparing for a court case with Humphries he changed his plea to guilty a day before the trial. The court handed down a sentence of three years and nine months, though I think some of it was suspended. The police officers told me that Humphries was visibly shocked when he heard the verdict. I had not spoken to him since the telephone call we had on the day he committed his crime. When the dust had settled I had lost a total £2.3 million in cash. I had sold my Liffe shares cheaply and lost all the premium and goodwill I had previously had for the business. The goodwill was the premium over and above the company's assets that I could have obtained if I had sold the company as a going concern. You could say I lost about £7 million.

The time had come to pay my £600,000 and formally join the GHF board. But stumping up that sort of money would mean swallowing up all the cash I had left. I no longer had the appetite for it. It just did not seem worth the risk anymore. I told Wenman I had decided not to join. He said that he did not want to be a partner either without me involved. I repaid his £600,000 and he walked away. He had lost a grand total of £400,000 believing in me and he never moaned once. I felt terrible and part of me wanted to give him the rest of his money back. But I had already suffered enough and he knew the risks of the business. He was a true gentleman. The directors at GHF understood when I told them that I was going to walk away from the business. GHF had not done badly out of the deal. My traders and brokers were now generating a large proportion of their income and they had not had to pay a penny for their services. Sussex Futures had been their biggest competitor so the fact that we were out of business did not hurt either. I told GHF that I could not stay on as an employee after I had previously been the owner of the business. Gedon Hertshten, the chairman and owner of GHF, agreed so I walked away. My time in the City looked like it had come to an end.

14

Liffe After the Floor

The rogue trading of Humphries had almost ruined me and all my staff and traders had lost their jobs. We were not the only people facing an uncertain future at this time. The last of the trading pits on the Cannon Bridge floor closed almost a year after the rogue trading incident on 2 May 2000, leaving a final band of the exchange's options dealers to hang up their coloured trading jackets for the last time. Many were surprised at the quickness of the floor's death. One dealer would lament 'We knew how good we had it on the floor, but the speed of the closure caught many of us out. One minute we were going to [a new exchange at] Spitalfields, the next minute we were starting a whole new life – with just the one f.' Some floor workers had been made redundant on the spot without any notice. Such was the fear among banks closing their floor operations that a disgruntled employee might engage in some rogue trading. There was no template for what ex-floor workers would go on to do. Some American traders including LaPorta returned to the US and worked at the CME. Others started a new life down under working at the Sydney Futures Exchange in Australia.

There are not too many working environments which can match the unique milieu of a trading floor. A generation of traders had made the Cannon Bridge floor their home. Most runners had marked out their territory with posters of their favourite football club, a picture of a desired sports car or favourite Page Three model from *The Sun* newspaper in the administration booths. Everyone knew the rules of the game in the pits. You could lark around as much as you liked and even take a two-hour lunch when dealing was quiet as long as total commitment was given when the trading floor got busy. If that meant working a 12-hour day all week, so be it. Adapting to the normality of a nine-to-five job could be very difficult. Some would find the constraints of sitting behind an office desk almost unbearable. One ex-trader said he constantly had to stand up and walk around the office as he adjusted to his new life. Other ex-traders struggled with the responsibility of working as a manager. Being responsible for dozens of employees could be quite a change from just worrying about how you performed in the pits each day.

Legends of the Cannon Bridge jungle were left feeling like dinosaurs wandering in the wilderness with nowhere left to go. Apart from at a few smaller venues such as the International Petroleum Exchange (IPE), open outcry had become extinct in the City. Electronic trading had made floor traders surplus to requirements. Their fate was not dissimilar to that of a coal miner who was the best in the business at digging coal out of the ground before a machine came along and did the job 10 times quicker, leaving the honed craft of coal digging obsolete. Some dealers would have to cope with going from earning half a million pounds a year to next to nothing. Ex-floor workers who tried to continue working in the City were often told by potential employers that they were either too old or too experienced. Most dealers were ill-prepared for the new computerised age of electronic trading. The exchange fell well short of providing the level of training which was needed for traders to feel comfortable using a computer. When Liffe had introduced the after-hours electronic APT system it exposed the shortcomings that many dealers had when it came to using new technology. One trader picked up his mouse and tried to talk to it when inputting the day's trades into the APT system for the first time.

Most of the floor workers that attempted to make the transition to screen-based trading failed. Many had started their careers at Liffe in their early twenties when the exchange first opened and were in their late thirties when the floor closed. This generation were not at ease with using computers. While e-mail has now become a ubiquitous communication tool, many of the floor workers that attempted to get to grips with screen-based dealing did not even own a PC. Dealers with sweaty palms would nervously tap the keypad and click their mouse to make their first trades on-screen. There were quite a few incidents of so-called fat fingered trades, which involve a trigger-happy dealer unwittingly executing a multitude of trades instead of one single transaction. This usually occurred when a dealer clicked the right button on a mouse rather than the left. While the left button allowed the trader to join the bid or offer, the right button sold directly into the bid or purchased the offer, establishing a position opposite to the one the trader wanted. Some did not find the hand–eye coordination needed to master control of these opposing functions easy to master. One trader who made such an error received a telephone call from his risk manager asking him why he was selling so much. 'What is your information?' he was asked. When the dealer replied that he was not selling he was horrified to learn that he was in fact selling everything in the market! A highly successful local who had made millions in the market chose to employ a person who sat next to him and inputted the trades for him on the screen. He was far too technophobic to click the mouse and make the trades himself. Terry Crawley did not bother at all with screen-based trading and instead moved into the world of property speculation. Quite a few ex-Liffe dealers started to build up property portfolios, buying houses in the Essex and Kent area.

There was a feeling among locals who made the transition to trading on screens that the odds had become stacked against them. In the pits, everyone could see what was happening. The shouts and hand movements of other traders revealed the positions, trading styles and emotions holding sway in the market. These signs of activity were blurred out of focus on the screens, making it far more difficult for dealers to interpret the strategies of other traders. The camaraderie of the floor was lost. Traders instead walked into the offices of brokerage firms which were sometimes inhabited by just a handful of dealers. Alone at their desks, many traders became quite lonely and introspective. The buzz of stepping on to a heaving trading floor was just a memory from a past world. Dealers sat in front of a screen with their headphones on, lost in their own thoughts. Conversations were limited to those with people seated nearby. A whole day could go by without speaking to anyone. This made trading more perilous as, unlike on the floor, traders missed out on the chance of obtaining some helpful advice from other dealers. Locals trying their hand at screen trading would lose money and pack it in only to return to have another go a few months later. Trading was the only job these dealers knew how to do, despite being ill-equipped to succeed in the new electronic age. Another £10,000 would be deposited with a broker to set up an account, only for the money to vanish a few months later. Some locals would keep coming back to have another go at trading until a savings pot was emptied and they were forced to look for work elsewhere or find a proprietary trading and clearing firm which would sponsor them to trade. These firms would be able to claw the money back from a sponsored trader through fees and commission charges. Some of the ex-Liffe dealers that did become successful day traders are still plying their trade in the City, renting desks at independent dealing firms known as trading arcades.

While electronic trading provided the big banks with greater transparency and anonymity it also gave them more opportunities to unleash financial juggernauts into the market which could swallow up the new army of screen traders, leaving them nursing losses. A wealthy dealer based in Switzerland who was known as 'The Flipper', became the nemesis of many traders. The Flipper traded the Bund, Bobl contracts on the DTB and the Euribor on Liffe. He specialised in trading in two different markets and would routinely flip a bid on thousands of futures contracts into an offer. The Flipper would spoof a large bid and put a small offer into the markets. Locals would buy the offer with the belief that there was a large buyer in the market.

After the Flipper had sold to the locals he would then pull his bid and 'flip' it into an offer on the offer price. Rather than making money from large City institutions, the Flipper specialised in taking money out of the pockets of the locals. His identity was eventually discovered after he attended a Liffe function and he received death threats from screen traders who had lost money as a result of his actions.

Floor brokers at major investment banks who had enjoyed annual salaries of £100,000 made the mistake of starting new lives as day traders when the pits closed. A £40,000 redundancy payment would be used to set up a trading account at a brokerage firm. These day traders had a good understanding of the fundamentals of the market. Floor brokers would speak at length with dealers from investment funds and bank proprietary trading desks about the ebb and flow of the markets. This gave them an intimate knowledge of the behaviour of various financial instruments and the impact of economic and geopolitical events on dealing at major exchanges. But these dealers were still novices when it came to trading with their own money. Edwin Lefèvre's classic tome *Reminiscences of a Stock Operator*, which was first published in 1923, summed up the difficulties such 'ghost gamblers' had when their own money was put on the line. 'It is like the old story of the man who was going to fight a duel the next day,' wrote Lefèvre.

His second asked him, 'Are you a good shot?'
'Well,' said the duelist, 'I can snap the stem of a wineglass at twenty paces,' and he looked modest.
'That's all very well,' said the unimpressed second. 'But can you snap the stem of the wineglass while the wineglass is pointing a loaded pistol straight at your heart?'

Put in front of trading screens, ex-floor brokers were unable to pull the trigger. The money in their trading accounts slowly trickled away. These dealers could not cope with the sight of seeing a personal savings pot being whittled away on the back of a market move. This made many of these day traders panic and close out positions at a loss. A good professional trader needs the confidence and speed of thought to make the right split-second decision as prices move. Ex-floor brokers would discover that no amount of financial and economic knowledge would compensate for not having the instinct to make the right decision when the heat was on. Within six months a £40,000 redundancy payment would be chopped down to just £15,000. Most executed dealing strategies which were far too conservative and risk averse. The fear of losing money resulted in them dying a slow death before they belatedly realised that the job of a professional trader was not for them.

Even highly successful bank traders that set up personal dealing accounts just to provide themselves with a boost to their retirement income were unable to trade well with their own money. A top trader at a US investment bank who retired as a multi-millionaire at the age of 37 opened a £50,000 trading account with a brokerage firm. He made just £3,000 in six months. While he would think nothing of buying 1,000 lots of futures contracts in his previous incarnation at the US investment bank's proprietary trading desk even he found himself unable to pull the trigger. This was what separated bank traders from the best locals who would be unflinching in their conviction of where the market was heading and risk large sums of their own money to back up their belief. The ex-Liffe workers that failed as professional traders often ended up looking for work outside the industry.

Quite a few marriages broke up after the floor closed. Being the wife of a successful Liffe trader could be enough to get on the guest list of a whole host of celebrity parties. Wives of traders forged friendships with the B and C-list celebrities of the day. As often as not these trophy wives disappeared not long after the pits closed and their husbands found themselves out of work. I know several great traders who are now divorced and living in bedsits while driving a mini-cab to make ends meet. The glamorous ex-wife made sure that she and the children kept the £1 million home.

The brash way of life enjoyed by many of the younger pit traders did not come cheap. The closure of the floor could mean the end of a lavish lifestyle of fast cars, beautiful women, designer suits and Rolex watches. Being a top Liffe trader provided a lifestyle that was on a par with being a Premiership football player at the time. One trader on the floor regularly socialised with 'the spice boys', a group of Liverpool football players in the mid-nineties that included Robbie Fowler, Steve McManaman, Stan Collymore, Jamie Redknapp, David James and Jason McAteer. When the trader was with the players and chatting up a young beauty at a nightclub he joked that she was spending her evening with the rich and famous. 'I'm rich and they're famous,' he quipped. The closure of the floor could mean the end of the dream. Some guys who had been doing regular jobs before getting a lucky break on the Liffe floor found themselves reapplying for work with their old employers. A few traders lost the discipline of being able to control their finances on a modest income and ended up filing for bankruptcy. Others resorted to crime and spent time in jail. Some even committed suicide.

The melting pot that was the Liffe floor has never since been replicated in the City. London's financial district remains an elite world inhabited by people of wealth and power. While the banter on bank trading floors is still fierce, the only time you are likely to see an ex-building site worker or market trader around is when there is a maintenance job which needs attending to. A stint at Sussex Futures would be the only job in high finance that some of my dealers ever had. One trader, who was known as El Pel or Chief – a nickname he earned through a habit of calling everyone 'chief' – had worked on a building site before he got a job on the floor by word of mouth. The quick-witted Chief proved himself to be a good order filler. But he did not possess the skills needed to become a top trader. When the floor closed he went back to work on the building site, grateful for the experience of being a derivatives dealer. A broker who worked for me in the Eurolira pit, went on to become a postman. This would be a lifestyle choice. He enjoyed not having to work under pressure and he was able to collect his children from school every day. The broker had paid off his mortgage and had put enough savings in the bank to ensure that he would never have to worry about money again. Macca, who worked for me in the Bobl pit, took about seven years to carve out a new life after the floor closed. He had spells of unemployment and even took on a job as a scaffolder – a desperate move considering his terror of heights. A friend who owned a building company hired him and arranged for Macca to only work on bungalows and low-level buildings.

A few of the 'barrow boy' characters that traded at the exchange went back to work on market stalls. John Jones became a fish monger at Billingsgate market. The black-haired Jones was in his mid-forties at the time but he had a stocky build and could easily handle hard manual work. I had employed Jones as an order filler for Sussex Futures in the Bund pit during his last three years on the exchange. Jones had specialised in using charting techniques to look for break-out points in the market during his career as a local and had earned a six-figure salary. During the nineties he had enjoyed the lifestyle of a top earner in high finance, splashing out on the best designer suits and eating in some of London's top restaurants. Working at the bustling East London fish market must have been quite a culture shock for him as fish mongers usually have to wake up at about two o'clock in the morning to start work on time. At the market you will find barrow boys making their way around lanes with trolleys filled with just about every variety of fish that you can imagine. Jones was quoted in a newspaper article comparing the principles which governed the fish market with those of the Liffe floor. 'If there are lots of seagulls around, that usually means that there is bad weather on the coast, so there isn't much cod, so you'll go long on cod. Or in a certain month there might be a run on haddock because everyone has suddenly discovered a new recipe,' he said.

There are a few ex-traders now earning a living as professional gamblers. Sports betting was always a part of the culture at Liffe. Dealers would often make a few bets on the horses when business was quiet on the floor. One former Liffe employee compared working the courses as a professional horse racing gambler with his old career on the Liffe floor. 'You have the rogues, the rumours, the Hooray Henrys, the sharks. You build a book, watch how it goes, pay, have a few drinks, build another book. You even have the hand signals,' he told a journalist after the exchange floor closed. Pit traders took techniques from the floor and applied them to sports betting. While electronic dealing was making the financial markets increasingly efficient, anomalies still existed in the nascent world of sports betting. Ex-traders would scan the odds offered by different bookmakers and lay bets arbitraging between the different prices available. While punters would be betting on their favourite sports team to win, the old Liffe dealers were trading like a bookmaker, scrutinising the prices and momentum in different markets and taking long and short positions accordingly. One ex-trader is rumoured to be making about £100,000 a month from sports betting. When I had a pint with Dogsy recently, he told me that he was earning a living gambling on the horses on Betfair.com, the online betting exchange.

A select few would successfully make the transition to screen-based trading or carve out a lucrative second career in the City. Those most likely to succeed on the screens were the young yellow-jacketed clerks who never got a chance to trade on the floor. These guys were far hungrier to learn how to trade on screens than the older guys. They also did not have the handicap of having any bad habits. Experienced traders that stayed in the industry were more likely to move into IT or back office support jobs at banks. For example, Lama (Andy Hughes) became far more interested in the technology of dealing than trading itself and went on to work as an IT manager after his career on the floor ended.

A notable success story from the dealing pits was that of Tom Theys. The American, who had a crew cut of short dark brown hair, learned how to trade in the pits of Chicago at the CBOT. He was one of the first Americans to work on the Liffe floor at the Royal Exchange and he played an active part in the workings of the exchange, serving on floor committees. His modest success in the dealing pits made him known as the 100 tick-a-day man. He used scalping techniques to make £1,000 each morning in the Bund pit. This would usually be done by trading between 300 and 600 contracts within two hours. As soon as he had achieved his goal he would leave the floor for the day. I would often pass him walking down the stairs near the reception of the exchange. He would usually have a smile on his face as he left early in the afternoon. 'Made the 100 ticks then Tom?' I would ask. While we all thought that he spent his afternoons away from the exchange playing golf, Theys was in fact developing trading computer software. In the mid-nineties he founded Patsystems. The venture aimed to develop hand-held devices which would allow pit traders on the Liffe floor to put orders into other markets, primarily the DTB. Floor traders would have been able to use the technology to pursue arbitrage strategies between London and Frankfurt. But Liffe would not allow Liffe traders to use such hand held devices in the pits. The exchange would not even allow the technology to be integrated with its after-hours APT platform. Theys then focused his efforts on developing software which would allow dealers to obtain direct access to exchanges over the internet. Liffe's arch enemy, the DTB, became Patsystems first customer before a host of other continental exchanges wired up to the technology to increase dealing volumes. Patsystems soon became a leading internet software vendor when Investec, which specialises in taking technology companies public, approached the company. The South African bank oversaw an initial public offering (IPO) on the London Stock Exchange for the company in March 2000 which raised about $80 million. In 2003, Patsystems listed on London's AIM market. Theys left the company a very wealthy man in the same year. Patsystems has since become a leading global provider of trading systems to derivatives traders.

Another Cannon Bridge visionary was Phil Docker. The portly Docker wore spectacles and liked to go to spend his lunchtimes having some banter in the pub with the chaps that worked for him. He was not the sharpest dresser on the floor and was never an outstanding dealer. Docker could easily have passed unnoticed among the thousands of traders that worked in the Cannon Bridge pits. But Docker was smart enough to see where the future of trading was heading. He left Liffe a couple of years before the floor closed with Paul Varcoe, who became his business partner. Varcoe had served as head options trader for Salomon Brothers while Docker worked as his futures broker at the exchange. The pair founded EasyScreen in 1998, which provided trading software to screen-based traders. The pair convinced leading investment banks such as Deutsche Bank and JP Morgan to use the technology. An IPO saw EasyScreen become listed on London's AIM market and the company was worth about

£140 million in 2000. But the bursting of the dot.com bubble whittled the share price down to pennies. The pair made a relatively modest sum of a few million pounds when the business was sold to Refco in 2005.

Docker supported Manchester United and he was also a big fan of Italian football and would take clients to Milan's San Siro stadium to watch AC Milan or Internazionale play. Flying out to Italy to watch a Serie A match was particularly popular among Liffe traders in the eighties when the Italian first division was the best football league in the world. Docker captained an EasyScreen football team which played against a Liffe Old Boys team which included Dickinson and was captained by myself. The match took place on the hallowed Wembley turf in the same year that the floor closed. Both teams had to stump up £12,500 each for the privilege of taking part in one of the last matches to be played at the old stadium before it was completely rebuilt. When we ran out of the Wembley tunnel and onto the pitch in the empty stadium we were greeted by the roar of a CD recording of the Wembley crowd which blared out of the stadium's loud speakers to give the game a big-match feel. The only real-life spectators were a small gathering of wives, friends and children of the players. A newspaper article covered the match under the headline: 'You thought it was all over? It is now.' Docker told the journalist that he had been dreaming about the match for months while gasping on a cigarette during a spell on the substitute's bench. He had even gone on a three-month diet in preparation for the game, which trimmed his waist down from 38 inches to 32 inches. 'I've saved so much money I may have turned in a profit on the whole thing,' he said while patting his stomach. Unfortunately, even a slim line Docker was not enough to win the day for the EasyScreen boys. We thrashed them 5-0. My son, Paul, grabbed two of our goals. I had the honour of climbing the steps to the Royal Box where Elizabeth Richard, a royal looka-like, handed out our winning medals. Here I lifted a replica of the FA Cup to celebrate our victory. Docker would leave the stadium a happy man with a plastic cup containing a divot of turf from the Wembley pitch.

A bronze statue erected in 1997 to mark the fifteenth anniversary of Liffe is the last remaining symbol of the army of floor workers that once inhabited the Cannon Bridge floor. The bronze cast, which stands on the corner of Walbrook and Cannon Street, has been carved into the image of a young dealer who strikes a pose while his ear is pressed towards a brick-sized mobile phone. The sculptured figure has a smile on his face, which suggests he has enjoyed another winning day in the pits. Ex-floor traders still pop by some of the pubs near the exchange to have a few beers and reminisce about the old days. You might be able to spot them in a crowded bar by the hand signals which can be instinctively used when buying a round. Old habits die hard! Apart from being Essex boys armed with a few Italian-style hand gestures, the only thing ex-floor workers are likely to have is a bunch of memories of an era which is fast evaporating in the financial markets. Most view their time at the exchange with affection. As one ex-Liffe dealer put it 'Who else worked in one room with 4,500 other people, played football with paper and sellotape balls, pinned paper and cardboard d***s on each others' backs, sang and chanted at passers by (including political leaders) and had a job interview which meant a trip to the pub?'

15

The Last Hurrah

I was now on the edge of retirement. It had not been easy watching Sussex Futures fall apart after pouring my heart and soul into the business for all those years. I had put back on the weight that I had lost but I still felt wounded by the whole experience. It was hard work carving out a successful career in the financial markets when you are the son of factory worker who left school at the age of 16. I never had any illusions about how tough the world of business and money could be. But nothing could have prepared me for the disastrous series of events which the actions of Humphries had brought to my life.

My only connection with the City's square mile was a stake in easy2trade, an internet-based trading company. The start-up was launched in late 1999 at the height of the dot.com boom. The outfit had been put together by some big hitters in the City, including Docker, the owner of EasyScreen, Phil Barnett, the former head of Smith Brothers Futures and James Campbell-Grey, who formerly served as a director at Liffe before becoming head of futures at ICAP, the London-based interdealer broker. My trusted friend Wenman also had a stake in the business. I became a shareholder and non-executive director. The venture aimed to provide the man at home with the same dealing screen as the man at Goldman Sachs. I really believed that we had a great product and thought being first to market with the concept would put us in a very strong position. To make things better, I only had one board meeting a month to attend. This seemed an ideal arrangement for a quiet peaceful life, given the tumultuous events of the past few years.

During this time I had been sponsoring Mad Dog as a trader. Aside from helping out an old friend, I wanted to put something back into the local community in Basildon. But I had no idea how this could be done until one day it dawned on me that I could set up a trading arcade in Basildon. This would give young lads in the local community the opportunity to start a career in high finance. Mad Dog could start dealing at the new company while serving as the floor manager and I could do a deal with easy2trade to get cheap access to the market while beta testing its system. This left everyone a winner.

E-Local Trading opened for business in July 2001. I had found office space in the heart of Basildon shopping centre and had recruited 10 raw trainees. All but one had come to me through word of mouth. David Barnett, former head of trading at Royal Bank of Canada and an old friend, introduced me to his ex-wife's stepson, Matt Blom, who became my first trainee. The others were local lads that knew my son or had a father that had worked with me in the City. The only exception was Ben Shaw, a devout orthodox Jew, who had responded to an advertisement which I had placed in a local newspaper.

I did not plan to devote too much time to the business. After spending the first few months setting everything up I planned to just pop in once a week to keep an interest in how things were developing. This was not the easiest time to teach novices how to trade on an internet-based system. The technology, media and telecoms (TMT) bubble had burst in 2000 and stock markets had been distinctly jittery since the spring. Then on 11 September 2001 two hijacked aeroplanes crashed into the twin towers. My team of traders was huddled around a TV screen in the office watching Sky News when the second plane crashed into the World Trade Centre. 'Oh my God, someone's declared war on America!' shouted the 23-year-old Blom. Everyone was in shock. Now my team of nine traders – with an average age of 21 and just three months' trading experience – had to trade in conditions of unbridled panic in the financial markets. Thankfully, my experience from the crash of 1987 was an enormous help in guiding them all through. Traders are very vulnerable to suffering losses when they get caught in situations that they do not understand. I knew first-hand how quickly prices could move when an exceptionally unusual market event occurred. My team traded very cautiously and at the end of the day we did not get hurt financially.

The task of teaching my young recruits was made all the more difficult in the post-September 11 market landscape. The financial markets were edgy during the months after the terrorist attacks which made prices bounce around a lot. The fact that my traders were relying upon internet technology that was not up to the job did not make things easier. We simply did not have the bandwidth or speed that a professional trading room requires. The internet model which easy2trade pioneered would later be a huge success for dealing firms such as GNI, deal4free and IG Markets. Business school professors could use the story of easy2trade as an example of when being first to the market is not an advantage. All the big retail brokers did not want to see their commission diminish which meant that they were not keen to offer the service to their customers. The teething problems inherent in the technology – which were mainly the result of poor internet connections – and the bursting of the dot.com bubble made it impossible for easy2trade to raise more capital. This meant we all lost our money. The venture cost me £100,000.

E-Local was my last remaining venture. But making it a success was not going to be easy. In the end, Mad Dog chose to leave. The guys begged me to take over after his departure. Reluctantly, I agreed. I was back in the business again. This time my days were spent imparting my knowledge to a young team of traders that were hungry to learn. I made sure that they learnt the craft of never speculating and always making sure that the risk/reward ratio was in their favour. Buy cheap and sell expensive was the mantra. I imparted the full repertoire of skills that a trader needs, teaching them how to scalp, spread and look for value in the market. Slowly, we started to make progress. It felt quite rewarding seeing them develop their skills as traders. I could see myself in some of them. They had that hunger. Days off were never taken while weekends were spent reading about trading and furthering their knowledge of the financial markets. A win-at-all costs culture blossomed. These boys would do whatever it took to succeed.

We specialised in trading Liffe's benchmark Euribor contract. This was my market. But in the new era of click-and-trade dealing, being over six foot tall with a loud voice did you no favours. Nevertheless, I had helped design the pro-rata trading algorithm for the Liffe Connect platform, which meant that I knew all about the advantages and disadvantages of trading on-screen. Not being able to see the flows in the market or who was doing business made guessing what other market participants were up to far more difficult. I was not in my comfort zone. It was not even possible to see who the counter-party was in a transaction. But my intuition for what was driving the market had not left me. Trading on-screen is also better than dealing on the floor for certain types of trades. For example, complicated dealing strategies on the floor such as inter contract spreads can be done seamlessly with a click of the mouse.

The so-called 'game boy generation' were taking over the markets. Sonny Schneider epitomised this new breed of technologically savvy dealer. He came into the market when the writing was on the wall for the floor. He chose to focus on screen-based trading and quickly become hugely successful. He set up Schneider Group in 1998 as a specialist electronic screen-based trading firm. Sonny approached me at a dinner held at the prestigious Mansion House venue in the City and asked if I would become a non-executive director of his business and I agreed. He had walked into my office four years earlier propos-ing a tie-up with his team of traders. This was at the same time that Humphries knocked on my door. I had turned Schneider down because I felt the deal he proposed was too aggressive and there was no profit margin in it for me. Now I had ended up working for him! I served my last three years in the business on the Schneider board.

During this time Sonny and I frequently had our disagreements but he always treated me with respect and I like the guy. Rival firms and even his own shareholders know what it is like to lock horns with him. He is a tough businessman and Schneider Group has turned out to be what Sussex Futures should have been.

While serving on the Schneider board I watched E-Local grow from next to nothing to become a force on the markets. I was able to recruit more traders and the business moved to an industrial estate in the local area, inhabiting 4,000 square feet of office space. Neighbours included major banks such as RBS and our dealing room was now comparable to that of major City institutions after a six-figure sum of trading profits was reinvested into the business. I now had a business with offices that were the same size as Sussex Futures when we were at our peak. Volumes and profits continued to grow and by 2006 E-Local had captured 6% of the Euribor market. This was not bad going for a bunch of kids from Basildon. Just five years earlier my team was learning the very basics of how to trade. Now they were pitting their wits against traders at Europe's biggest investment banks. While many of the recruits who walked through our doors would fail the business unearthed some great traders. Blom, my first signing, and Danny Hodgson became very talented. They would have been superstars in the age of open outcry. Adam Beckford, Luke Farrier, Andy Sully and Steve Hunter also excelled. I was proud of all of them.

Being the boss of a group of cocky young lads out to make a million in the financial markets did not come without its hazards. I liked to have a laugh and a joke with the best of them during my days in the pits but now I was the one in charge I could find myself on the receiving end of a few pranks. I walked into the office one morning and was shocked to discover that everyone had lost a fortune. Unbeknown to me, the risk screens had been tampered with. This was done just to see the look on my face when I saw the huge losses on the screens. It took several minutes before I realised that the date was 1 April. By this time the colour had drained out of my face as I surveyed the screens in horror. The April Fools' trick was more than a bit of a shock for me! But I had to take it.

While the September 11 terrorist attacks had left my young team of dealers scrambling to survive everyone would be much better prepared when terrorists struck much closer to home four years later. News of the suicide bomb attacks on the London transport system on 7 July 2005 quickly filtered to my dealers via a news feed which the company had set up. While the immense bravery of London's emergency services on that day puts the whole world of the capital markets in perspective, I was pleased that my traders had matured enough to deal professionally with such an unexpected event. The firm made profits of about £100,000 on the day but no one felt like celebrating given the tragic loss of life which had taken place.

The success of E-Local had proved that I did have what it took to succeed in the new electronic age. I had set up a business from scratch and turned it into a success. Now I really was ready to retire. In March 2007 at the age of 48 I called it a day after a career which spanned three decades in the financial markets. Perhaps I got out at the right time! Technology is developing at such a breakneck pace now. Where this is taking the financial world and global economy, I am damned if I – or anyone else for that matter – really know. If you pick up the newspaper tomorrow and see a near record jump or fall in a major financial index, it will just be the latest spasm. Financial markets are shaking as much as the elderly clearing bank dealer's 'cardiac chart' trading card when he ventured down to the floor! The pace of dealing in the capital markets has been supercharged by automated electronic trading.

Things were very different all those years ago when I began my career at Cocoa Merchants. In those days, using a calculator was about as high-tech as it got and all trading was carried out over the telephone or on the exchange floor. When Cocoa Merchants put its trading ledgers on to a computer in the late seventies the hardware cost a small fortune. It took up more space than the entire accounts department and had much less power than a single laptop of today. While computers were already being used to execute trades in the seventies and eighties – some stock market analysts blamed programme trading for triggering the crash of 1987 – most stock brokers and dealers were still relying on manual processes to execute trades.

When the APT system was first introduced at Liffe in 1989 it simply provided a matching system for getting in and out of trades. Few people thought that it would be able to replicate the open outcry system.

However, the base emotions of fear and greed rule the market in just the same way today as they did when I started my career as a trader in the seventies. Walk on to the trading floor of a major bank or broker just before the release of an important piece of economic data or in the aftermath of a major world event and you will sense the same rush of excitement which gripped traders in the old days of the Liffe floor. Traders still rely on charts to project where prices are heading and make decisions based upon the fundamental economic laws which make markets tick.

Many of today's professional traders also have the same ethos as those of my generation. An old friend from my days on the floor went to a beach party in Gibraltar which had guests from both the old and new generation of trading. 'When it comes to traders, let's just say life is unchanged,' he said. The young guns showed just as much enthusiasm for enjoying the fruits of their labour as we did. But the skill set which a trader now needs is changing. Being tough with a quick-thinking mind is not so important in an increasingly virtual world where flickering numbers on computer screens move markets across the globe. The primeval skill of looking into the eyes of another dealer and anticipating his thoughts no longer has any place in the markets. The sanitised, soulless world of electronic trading is a far cry from the dealing pits where traders with strong personalities used a loud voice and brute strength to get an edge.

The rise of algorithmic trading and 'black box' technology – in which computerised mathematical algorithms are used to power dealing strategies independent of the human hand – is increasingly making the role of the professional trader obsolete. TABB Group, a financial technology consultancy firm, predicted that by 2009 algorithmic trading will account for half of all equity trading in the US. These computer programmes execute the same types of trades that dealers did on the floor – but at a much faster pace. This is making speed of thought a less prized commodity – man can never be faster than machine. World chess champion Garry Kasparov's shock defeat to Deep Blue, a super computer developed by IBM, gave the world an early warning of the new paradigm that is emerging. Kasparov was able to come back from his defeat in 1997 and claim a draw against Deep Junior (another computer chess programme) in a 'Man vs Machine' match in January 2003. But the odds are increasingly staked against man in his battle with ever more powerful machines. A fact the professional trader is all too aware of. The craft of spreading between contracts to get an edge, looking for opportunities to scalp and finding value in trades cannot yield the rewards that it did in my days on the floor. Technology has made the markets far more efficient. Left without an edge, a dealer is forced to take an outright position in the market and speculate on prices going one way or another. As is the case with the average crowd at the bookies on a Friday afternoon, when you see a group of speculators on the markets the only safe bet is that most will be losers. I was a professional trader; never a gambler. Guys like me provided liquidity on the exchange. We took advantage of any value in the market by doing our homework to find out what was cheap and expensive, before trading the minimum price movement – up or down – in the market. We traded quickly in response to market data and breaking news events. I have never believed that I know more about the direction of where the market is heading than anyone else. Only geniuses and fools think they do. I do not know too many geniuses.

Few of today's generation of traders will have started working in the City straight out of school like I did. Some will have even spent five years studying for a PhD in mathematics or physics. A new breed of IT-literate traders are increasingly finding work navigating complex computer dealing programmes. These systems do everything from trading in response to news events – which are transmitted to them in milliseconds via computer code – to slicing and dicing massive market orders into small chunks. The traders that operate these dealing algorithms need a mind which understands the complexity of the trades which these programmes churn out. This ability is very different to the skills needed by traders on the exchange floor, who made many decisions in a short space of time. Rapid-fire decisions of the type taken in the pits are made by machines now. Screen traders are finding themselves unable to pull off trades that were possible just three years ago. For example, traders are no longer using calculators in dealing rooms to work out the differential in the price on the bid offer spread of contracts. So-called statistical arbitrage programmes are cleaning these types of transactions up in milliseconds.

An unexpected consequence of the emergence of IT specialist traders has been that the trading floor has made a comeback. Only this time it is the racks of computer servers at exchanges and not a crowd of coloured-jacketed dealers that are driving trading volumes. The CME's floor may now be just sparsely populated with a few options dealers. But the exchange floor has become a nexus for cables pumping data at breakneck speeds to the four corners of the earth. Trading firms are installing computer servers at exchanges to enhance the speed at which trades can be executed in the market. So-called proximity hosting services are being offered by exchanges such as the CME, Eurex and Liffe, which pump data from exchanges down pipes to banks and trading companies across the globe. Instead of data being transmitted within 100 milliseconds it is fired out to dealers in less than 5 milliseconds. In the age of algorithmic trading, he who is quickest usually wins. The faster a trader can obtain information on price data and act upon it the better. Point-and-click dealers attempting to exploit short-term market moves without high-speed connections to trading hubs are left chasing ghosts of prices which no longer exist. When the pits died some traders fantasised about dealing from a beach in Barbados, armed with just a laptop. The dream was to make a fortune while topping up a suntan. This fantasy may have become reality for some lucky dealers who wait years or months for trades to come off. But any dealer looking to exploit short-term fluctuations in the market in this way would have more luck trying instead to get a suntan on a beach in Skegness, a seaside resort in the north of England.

A consequence of the technological arms race taking place in the capital markets has been soaring dealing volumes in recent years. Liffe traded a billion contracts in a single year for the first time in

2008. The 1.05 billion contracts represented a 10.6% increase in trading volumes from 2007. However, at the time of writing trading volumes had dropped in the wake of the financial crisis. But the high levels of volatility in the financial markets remain. This has left incumbent exchanges like the London Stock Exchange creaking to process the millions of buy and sell orders rushing through their books when markets get wild. Embarrassing 'outages' at the established exchanges – where trading stalls – serve only to feed business at newly emerging alternative trading venues such as the London-based Chi-X. These platforms target the very generation of super-fast algorithmic traders which is taking the capital markets into the future. Could the LSE's domination of the share dealing of listed companies in London suffer the same fate as Liffe when it was forced to relinquish control of dealing in the Bund to the DTB when the Frankfurt-based exchange jumped ahead with a new electronic platform? This seems very unlikely at the moment. But as the events of 2008 prove, nobody is untouchable in the financial world now.

What is beyond any doubt is that levels of risk in global finance are on the rise. While barrow boys running wild on the dealing room floor may have made a good story in the popular press, even the most moronic rogue trader would struggle to do as much damage as is possible with computer-powered trading machines. I had only retired from the business a few months when markets across the world were sent into palpitations by malfunctioning computer trading programmes in August 2007. While financial experts are still not certain exactly what happened that August it is clear that unprecedented levels of volatility in the market and a subsequent leap in trading volumes were too much for some algorithmic trading programmes to handle. Since it was not possible for human traders to copy how these algorithms rapidly slice and dice orders, the breakdown of the computer programmes resulted in some dealing firms being unable to trade. Also, some algorithms fed off each other, forcing prices up or down, before they were switched off.

Problems occur with computer trading programmes when the rules of the trading and investment game change. When financial markets enter unchartered territory a machine will only be able to analyse the market based upon information from what has happened in the past. In these circumstances, it is arguably better to have a human making trading decisions based upon his intuition of what to do. Of course banks are in a technology arms race to produce platforms which can process ever larger amounts of trades in a shorter space of time. None are going to risk losing their edge in electronic markets by scaling back their dependence on cutting edge trading technology. But the impact of algorithmic trading models malfunctioning can result in banks suffering huge trading losses or financial indexes plummeting to depths that wipe billions of dollars off the value of listed companies in the real economy.

A leading expert in algorithmic trading technology at Lehman Brothers, the most high-profile victim of the credit crisis, was reported early in 2008 as saying that the Wall Street bank worried about the computer 'going wild and going off on its own ...' That was of course before the investment bank's exposure to sub-prime debt put it out of its misery. A specialist at another Wall Street firm, which is still trading, said volatile markets in August 2007 had made the bank completely rethink its plans for dealing with jumps in trading volumes. Instead of having a contingency plan for double the amount of trades in a single day the bank was preparing for a leap of 10 times the size of a typical day's trading. Will such measures be enough to protect the markets from the march of the machines? Who knows? What is certain is that financial markets will become increasingly dependent on computers to execute trading strategies while the number of professional traders dwindles.

Meanwhile, the great financial crisis of 2008 shows how technology is increasingly linking financial markets together in a way which can leave investment banks toppling like domino pieces when the complex financial instruments being traded blow up. But it is important to understand that the credit crunch was caused by bespoke over-the-counter (OTC) derivatives products which were packaged by greedy bankers. These products were tied to sub prime mortgages, often taken out by overindebted borrowers in the US who were turned away from the high street banks when applying for a loan. When these borrowers started defaulting on their home loans the value of the OTC products held on the books of investment banks plummeted as well. The credit risk of the products we traded was guaranteed by the exchange which meant the products never went into default. When used properly, exchange-traded derivatives actually reduce financial risks. For example, an airline company may protect itself against a rise in fuel prices later in the year by obtaining oil futures contracts at an exchange in New York which provide the company with a guaranteed price for the oil it needs that year. As Local traders, we provided a great service to financial institutions by supplying liquidity to the market and enabling them to protect themselves against financial risks. It was greedy bankers that risked our savings and pensions by using derivatives as supped-up gambling tools. Nobody else.

I can only feel privileged to have had the opportunity to be a trader on the floor of the Liffe exchange. There are not too many other examples in the history of finance where a bunch of working class guys with the balls to put their own money on the line were able to single-handedly build a major global financial institution. The dealing pits could be a ferocious place to earn a living but I loved every minute. I feel sorry for the current generation of traders that never got the chance to participate in such an enthralling experience. Every day was a pleasure.